The Seven Pillars of
FATHERHOOD

A Godly Seven-Point Guide for All Real Men When They Take on the Joys and Challenges of Fatherhood

Donald H. Wood, Ph.D

ISBN 978-1-63814-151-8 (Paperback)
ISBN 978-1-68526-115-3 (Hardcover)
ISBN 978-1-63814-152-5 (Digital)

Copyright © 2021 Donald H. Wood, Ph.D
All rights reserved
First Edition

All rights reserved. No part of this publication may be reproduced, distributed, or transmitted in any form or by any means, including photocopying, recording, or other electronic or mechanical methods without the prior written permission of the publisher. For permission requests, solicit the publisher via the address below.

Covenant Books, Inc.
11661 Hwy 707
Murrells Inlet, SC 29576
www.covenantbooks.com

In memory of Donald "Erik" Wood, my only begotten son, who departed this life far too soon as a result, in part, of my failure to grasp the fundamental values and attributes that make up what a real father must embrace in order to navigate fatherhood successfully. This includes piloting, providing, protecting, preparing, patience, and praying.

> He must manage his own family well and see that his children obey him, and he must do so in a manner worthy of full respect. (1 Timothy 3:4 NIV)

It is also my hope and prayer that this book will be not only instructional and inspirational but also a lasting legacy for all fathers now and in the future.

For my wife, Lydia, my constant companion, and one true love who is truly more than a conquer.
I have been put to proper use and made available for immediate use by my Lord and Savior Jesus Christ.

A wise servant takes charge of an unruly child
and is honored as one of the family.
—Proverbs 17:2

Wisdom has built her house; she has hewn out its Seven Pillars.
—Proverbs 9:1

CONTENTS

Acknowledgments 11
Introduction..13

Chapter 1:   The Importance of Fatherhood 17
Chapter 2:   Pillar 1—The Pilot Father..31
Chapter 3:   Pillar 2—The Provider Father 43
Chapter 4:   Pillar 3—The Protector Father 52
Chapter 5:   Pillar 4—The Preparing Father................................59
Chapter 6:   Pillar 5—The Praising Father 72
Chapter 7:   Pillar 6—The Patient Father....................................82
Chapter 8:   Pillar 7—The Praying Father...................................91

Survey Results and Analysis..101
Some Final Thoughts 109
Conclusion..117
Appendix: Fatherhood Survey 127
Suggested Reading..129

ACKNOWLEDGMENTS

I want to acknowledge and thank my family, friends, and neighbors who shared with me their thoughts and experiences. From your fatherhood survey responses, I gleaned invaluable insight into the subject of fatherhood and how each of your personal experiences and challenges with your fathers and father figures have impacted your lives.

INTRODUCTION

The most challenging and most rewarding thing a man can do in his life is to be a successful father. Yet so many men today, young and old, do not have a clue as to what or how to be a good much less a successful father. Unfortunately, fatherhood is not innate and not something we instinctively know how to do; it is a learned behavior.

Much has been written about what the role of a good father is and the importance of a father in his child's life. But little, if any, has been written about what the fundamental attributes are that make up a good or, what I like to call, a real father. I think that those fundamental attributes can be summed up with seven key traits or pillars, as I like to refer to them. Some men learn these traits from their biological fathers; others learn these traits from father figures in their lives, but in far too many cases, these fundamental traits are never learned to the detriment of far too many children.

To start any discussion on fatherhood, I think we first must define fatherhood. The dictionary defines fatherhood as "the state of being a father," "fathers collectively," "the qualities or spirit of a father," and "the kinship relation between an offspring and the father." But fatherhood is so much more than just the state of being a father, the qualities or spirit of a father, or the kinship between an offspring and the father. A father should be an active and willing participant in his child's life. Some even say that there is a difference between a father and a daddy. They argue that anyone can be a father, but it takes a special man to be a daddy. However, if you really think about it, a good father is a daddy, and a good daddy is a father. In today's culture, there are far too many young women classifying the men that fathered their children as "my baby's daddy" when what they are really saying is my baby's sperm donor. In order to be a real father, a man must adhere to fundamental truths that all good fathers have followed since the establishment of the family—fundamental truths that are founded and grounded in the Father of all fathers, our heavenly Father. These fundamental truths or attributes, as I stated above, are what I like to call the seven pillars (Ps) of fatherhood. They encompass the key attributes a good father should know. These are the following how-tos:

- Pilot or lead his family.
- Provide for his children.
- Protect his children.
- Prepare and teach his children about life.
- Be patient with his children.
- Praise/support his children.
- Pray for his children.

We all have heard of many of the negative terms for men that have nothing to do with their children such as sperm donor, deadbeat dads, and absentee father, just to name a few; all of which points to a serious flaw in today's society. It's unfortunate, but today, more than ever, we find men who father's one child after another without any regard for their well-being or proper upbringing. They don't have a clue as to what it takes to properly raise a child, much less what the fundamental pillars are of fatherhood that help to shape the future of his children for generations to come.

In addition, many of men's attitudes toward fatherhood today are shaped by what they see and learn from whatever father figure or image they had in their childhood no matter how flawed or detrimental that figure or image may have been.

They also form their attitudes about fatherhood from social media, the media in general, and from what they witness from past experiences of their peer group. They see rappers and famous celebrities jumping from bed to bed making baby after baby without a clue as to what it takes to be a real father. All the while, they are glorifying the idea that the more babies they have out of wedlock that are left to be raised by their mothers, grandparents, the government, or the streets is a way, somehow, to boost their egos. Any man can plant a seed, but it takes a real man to cultivate and nurture a seed until it blossoms into something that yields fruit a hundred times over.

So many kids today are bought up in families without a strong father figure; they are headed only by their mothers to the point that some women in today's culture feel it's a badge of honor to proclaim to the world that "I am a single mom" while the man that fathered their child is simply referred to as "my baby's daddy." They get caught up in the same cycle that perpetuates, what I like to call, the rolling stone syndrome, as defined by the once popular vocal group The Temptations in their song "Papa was a rolling stone and wherever he laid his hat was his home and when he left us all he left us was alone." To too many children, this is the image they have of a father or, should I say, the lack of a real father in their lives.

Because of this rolling stone attitude or sperm donor mentality, we now have a society full of kids that are brought up with no sense of conscience, no sense of right and wrong, no sense of how to love themselves, and even less sense of how to love their neighbor, have a total lack of moral values, and, most importantly, no sense of the Father of all creation, our Lord and savior Jesus Christ, who encompasses all of the above values and so much more. And in the words of the forty-fourth president of the United States, President Barack Obama, "We need fathers to realize that what makes you a man is not the ability to have a child, it's the courage to raise one."

This book, as stated above, explores not only the importance of fatherhood but also explores seven fundamental pillars of fatherhood. It supports and lends strength to a father that wants to raise a family that will produce successful and fruitful children. The value and importance of a father in a child's life can be seen in the following statistics:

- Seventy-two percent of the nation's teen murderers come from fatherless homes.
- Seventy percent of long-term prison inmates grew up in homes without fathers.

- Sixty percent of the people who commit rape were raised in homes where the father was absent.

I, for one, feel it's time to change these deplorable statistical numbers and pray that this book will be instrumental in its effort in changing the minds and hearts of what fatherhood really entails.

CHAPTER 1

The Importance of Fatherhood

One of the greatest needs of this age is for responsible and committed fathers.
—Bishop Charles Edward Blake Sr.

Most real men, particularly when their first child comes into the world have had the feeling of being overwhelmed and bewildered in the sense that they're thinking to themselves, *What the heck have I gotten myself into now?* The realization that they are now responsible for another human being and it's no longer just about them can hit home hard. However, this should be a time that they should be thinking about the importance of fatherhood and what it's going to take for them to be a successful father. And in order to be a successful father, they must, first and foremost, understand and realize that they must seek out and be led by the Holy Spirit—the father of all righteousness—if they want to become a successful father.

Why is the presence of a righteous and godly father so important to the family unit? To answer this question, lets first look at what happens without the presence of a godly father in a child's life and the family unit. To start, without a strong father image—an image formed in the likeness of all mankind, our heavenly Father—we are left with nothing more than distorted ideas and perceptions of what a real father looks like. It is a father figure that can be easily led and tempted by the enemy of all mankind, Satan, which can be detrimental in the development of morally and spiritually grounded children. For example, in the case of a male child without the proper father figure to model and emulate, the male child is left with trying to figure out how they are to carry themselves as a male seed. They are left with only the media, the streets, and whatever else the world and Satan suggest a father should be and look like. In other words, they are left with, in far too many cases, distorted ideals on how to accept responsibility, relate to and treat properly the opposite sex, manage money, raise their children, and, most importantly, look always to their heavenly Father for guidance and direction.

In the case of a female child without a strong Christ-centered father figure she too, as with her male counterpart, is left with the media and the world and Satan as her role model. It is also important to note that in the case of the female child, a father plays a special role in her life because he is her first example of how a man should treat a woman. If, for example, her father is abusive to her mother, then there is a high probability that she may engage in a relationship with an abusive male. In contrast, if she sees her father treating her mother with love, respect, kindness, and his queen, then it is likely she will seek out a man with the same traits and values. As Scripture states, "I would have you know that the head of every man is Christ; and the head of the woman is man; and the head of Christ is God." "Husbands love your wives, just as Christ loved the church and gave himself up for her" (Ephesians 5:25 NIV). Add to this fact that a man and woman become one once they are joined together in marriage, which means a man and a woman are now one flesh; why would a man not want to treat his wife (who is now part of his flesh) and God, who is his head, with love and respect?

In addition, a God-fearing, loving father can create in his daughter a strong sense of self-worth by telling her how beautiful and special she is. If this unconditional love and validation doesn't come from her father or a father figure in her life, she may seek it from a man, other than her father, who has, in many cases, hidden agendas that are self-serving and detrimental to her self-esteem. To quote John Eldredge in his book *Fathered by God*, "A girl learns if she is worth pursuing, if she is lovely, from her dad. That is just the way

God set this whole thing up. This power he has given to you." In far too many cases, you see young women who lack self-esteem to the point that they are exploited by not only self-serving husbands and boyfriends but, in some worst-case scenario, by pimps that exploit them for profit in the world of prostitution. It is every father's sovereign duty to protect his daughter not only physically but also emotionally by giving her his unconditional love, respect, and validation.

Speaking now from my own personal experience, I was, for the most part, especially in the early years of my life, brought up without a proper father figure to learn from, much less emulate. I didn't get a chance to live with my biological father until four years after my mother's death. I was only nine years old at the time of her passing. After my mother's passing and prior to me moving in with my biological father and his second wife (a woman who never had any children of her own but, as I learned later, had utilized abortion as a birth control method) on a permanent basis, I only knew him as the man who came to the house once a week to see my mother. I did not have any father-son relationship with him nor did I have enough encounters with him to emulate any of his behavior patterns. I was left with the task, after I became a father, of trying to figure out what was expected of or how to be a father based on the popular television shows of my childhood such as *Father Knows Best* and *Leave It to Beaver*. They were images of a culture and lifestyle that were pure fantasy in relationship to the extreme poverty I was experiencing at this time of my life. The only real-world father figure I could point to and emulate, after moving in with one of my older sisters and her husband, was my brother-in-law. Unfortunately, his example turned out to be one of a man that drank too much, beat his wife, and belittled and played favorites with his children. And to add insult to injury, the man was an atheist. In contrast to the brother-in-law that I was left to emulate and endure, my two younger sisters were blessed with a brother-in-law who was the total opposite. They moved to Dayton, Ohio, with my other older sister Laverne and her husband Sylvester. Her husband was a God-fearing, praying, real father figure in every sense of the word, and unlike my other brother-in-law, he embraced all seven pillars of fatherhood. He always put God, wife, children, and family first in his life. I wonder to this day how different my early childhood development would have been if he and my sister Laverne had taken me under their care along with my two younger sisters.

Even after I got married for the first time and subsequently sought the advice of and looked to my older brothers for examples to follow, I found myself even more confused and perplexed as to what it took to be a real father, more on the definition of a real father later. I say this because my oldest brother was an alcoholic, and his philosophy when it came to women was to seduce as many women as you could whether they were "eight to eighty, blind, cripple, or crazy." In addition, he could best be classified, in terms of fatherhood, as a revolving-door father, more on the classifications of what I like to call fake fathers' acronym later. In fact, to the best of my knowledge, he never stayed with one woman long enough to help in the rearing/raising of any of his children. Even more disturbing is the idea that in order to be a real man (notice I said real man not a real father), you should try to seduce as many women as you can while you are still young is still perpetuated. I say this because of a conversation my wife's uncle and brother had with her nephew concerning sex and women. They both are still perpetuating the same type of misleading philosophy that my oldest alcoholic brother once told me when I was a young unmarried man. They told my wife's nephew to seduce as many women as he can before he gets married—the continued unfortunate misguided belief of what makes up a real man.

My other brothers also had many distorted ideas concerning fatherhood and parenting. They too, based on their past experiences with other distorted father figures, had no clue as to what it really took to be a godly and spirit-filled father. For the most part, they felt if they provided their children with the basics, food and shelter, they had met their fatherly obligations. This idea that all I needed to do to fulfill my fatherly obligations is to simply make sure my kids are provided for—or in the words of far too many fake fathers, "My kids don't want for nothing"—is still the prevailing attitude of most men. This is what I discovered from statistical studies and the fatherhood survey that I conducted with my family, friends, and neighbors.

THE SEVEN PILLARS OF FATHERHOOD

I, along with my brothers, never imagined that to really father a child meant so much more than just the basics of food and shelter and that true fatherhood required a complete commitment to one's children and family. No one had ever demonstrated or taught us that we had to step up and be led by the Lord as the head or leader of our families, that we had to prepare and protect our children to go forth to be productive and fruitful citizens, that we had to be patient, praising/supportive, and loving so as to build a lasting relationship with them, and that we must always keep them lifted up in prayer.

I believe and have learned that the core value of any society begins and ends with the family unit. And at the center of that family unit is the father. According to Scripture, the family is the foundational institution of society ordained by God (Genesis 2:20–25 NIV).

Unfortunately, somehow, we have lost our way. We have lost our way to the point that the male seed is grossly out of position within the typical family unit. If you think this is not so, just look at the types of father images and alternative lifestyles our children are currently subjected to daily. Children are increasingly living in homes with unmarried parents, alcoholic parents, and being raised by grandparents. This fact was also revealed to be the case by the majority of the respondents who participated in my fatherhood survey.

To better understand what the traits and image of a good or, what I like to term, real father looks like, we must first look at the negative traits associated with the image of a bad father or, what I like to term, a fake father. These images can be seen in the following eleven negative traits I have outlined in the acronym for *fake fathers*.

The eleven negative traits are as follows:

F—fickle
A—arrogance
K—knave
E—evil inspired
F—false teacher
A—absenteeism
T—task master

H—high and mighty
E—egotistical
R—revolving door
S—softie

It's interesting to note that if these negative traits are not broken, they will be passed on to the next generation; they will perpetuate the ugly endless cycle of what can only be best described as "sperm donors" which leaves single moms to raise children on their own.

By way of example, I can remember from my own past experiences of being told and preached to by the father figures of my youth that it was okay to have a wife and a woman on the side as long as you paid your bills. Not realizing of course that a divided family is not a fully fulfilled family. Because when a man divides his time between his family and an outside affair, there will always be consequences. In addition, when a man spreads himself too thin, he runs the risk of destroying his family, and as Holy Scriptures tells us, you cannot serve two masters. You will either hate the one or love the other, or you will be devoted to the one and despise the other (Matthew 6:24 NIV).

I was also told it was okay to spend the bulk of my time running after the all mighty dollar while leaving the disciplining and rearing of my children to their mother; in the process I missed out on some of the most important and key events in my children's lives—events that included things like school plays, ball games, first day of school, graduations, and just spending quality time with them.

Too many men let their egos get the best of them when it comes to fatherhood responsibilities. They rely instead on how they were treated as a child as the template on how they are supposed to conduct themselves when it comes to raising their children.

Now let us take an even closer look at these eleven negative traits of a fake father. And even though I will refer to these fake fathers as men, they are nothing more than men-children. A man-child can best be described a male seed who acts like and runs away from his responsibilities like a child would but resides in a man's body.

THE SEVEN PILLARS OF FATHERHOOD

The negative traits of fake fathers can easily be summed up, as outlined above, by utilizing the following two acronyms: *fake* and *fathers*. The first letter *F* represents *fickle*. A fickle father trait can best be described as a man-child who, on the surface, appears to be operating like a real father but quickly changes whenever he is required to step up and be a real father (more on the definition of a *real* father later). He is the type that will tell his children one thing, but when pressed by them or their mother, he quickly gives in and lets his children do what they want instead of making them do what he knows is best for them. He is also the type who has unfair standards and is hypocritical. For example, he thinks it's okay for his son to sleep with as many girls as he desired, but when it comes to his daughter, he quickly flips the script and tells her she cannot sleep with or even think about sleeping with a boy until she is happily married. He is constantly confused as to the standards he should set for his family and what his role as a father should really look like.

The second letter *A* in the acronym fake represents *arrogance*. An arrogant father trait can best be described as a man-child who is overly aggressive in his approach to fatherhood. Even though he can visibly see that he has alienated his children with his overly aggressive style, he is too arrogant to change his approach. In addition, an arrogant father is a father that is unwilling to let his children make good choices on their own even though he may be dead wrong concerning how he feels about their decision. To put it simply, he is the type of father who is unwilling to take advice from anyone. For example, suppose his child wants and desires a career as a firefighter, but because there is a long tradition in the family that all the men follow a police officer's career path, his personal bias and arrogance causes him to push his child into a career they have no desire to pursue. I hope I am not dating myself too much, but I think a scene in the movie *An Officer and a Gentleman* best emphasizes this point. In the movie, aspiring young recruits are trying to get through boot camp and become navy pilots. As the movie progresses, we find that one recruit decides that the military career he was seeking was contrary to what he really desired to do with his life; he was only pursuing a career as a navy pilot because it was something his father wanted him to do. In the end, this dilemma causes him to take his own life. In other words, the bottom line with this trait is "my way or the highway." The Scriptures describe this as a man-child who has frustrated his children to the point he has lost touch with them based on his own selfish desires. "Fathers don't exasperate your children by coming down on them. Take them by the hand and lead them in the way of the Master" (Ephesians 6:4 MSG).

The third letter *K* in the acronym fake represents *knave* which simply means an unprincipled father trait. The unprincipled father figure has no sense of moral scruples, much less godly principles concerning fatherhood. They are the type of man-child who has no problem doing all kinds of ungodly and morally corrupt things around their children; they ignore the fact that they are their children's principal example on how to live their lives. For example, they are the type of man-child that will take their children on a rendezvous with another woman outside of their marriage or take them with them while they are out gambling and drinking. This kind of behavior is extremely impressionable on children, especially the younger child. They also subject their children to profane language and ungodly music; they then wonder why their children are displaying certain types of negative behavior, all of which their children imprinted from them. As the old saying goes, "Garbage in, garbage out." The Scripture describes this type of ungodly behavior as follows, "Do not let any unwholesome talk come out of your mouths, but only what is helpful for building others up according to their needs, that it may benefit those who listen" (Ephesians 4:29 NIV).

The fourth *E* in the acronym fake represents *evil-inspired*. The evil-inspired trait describes a man-child who is so caught up with evil deeds his children become nothing more than obstacles to the lifestyle he has chosen for himself—a lifestyle that is full of lying, cheating, stealing, adultery, and other evil deeds that will satisfy the lust of his flesh. It is a lifestyle that, at its core, is driven and orchestrated by the principal enemy of the flesh: Satan. This type of man-child will even teach his children deviant behaviors either by direct instructions or by modeling. In other words, this is a man-child who gravitates to all that is wrong in the world including how to raise his children.

The best example of this trait can be seen in the personas of mafia boss, pimp, drug dealer, or a corporate headhunter who puts profits above everything in life including their children. The scriptures best describe this as a man-child with no self-control. "A man without self-control is like a city broken into and left without walls" (Proverbs 25:28 NIV).

The fifth letter and the first letter *F* in the acronym for fake father represents *false teacher or prophet*. This trait describes a man-child who, by way of example, verbally teaches and preaches false ideals about fatherhood to his children. They teach and preach flawed ideals concerning how to discipline children, how to respect and relate to the opposite sex, how to conduct themselves with integrity and strength of character. In short, they teach and preach values that do not allow their children to become morally productive citizens. In addition, this trait can be devastating to a child's ego because what he thinks and says to his children can have a lasting impact upon them in profound ways. For example, if a man does not acknowledge his son or daughter as someone he can be proud of or if he is the type of man who doesn't reassure his children whenever they face setbacks in their lives, their self-esteem can be damaged for a lifetime. And in the case of the female child, their father must be the man that acknowledge their beauty and the main man in their lives that loves and reassures them unconditionally. However, if he fails to acknowledge them in these ways, there are always predators ready to seize the opportunity to jump into their lives with all types of ungodly hidden agendas; it bears repeating in the case of the male child that their father or father figure is first and foremost seen as their number one hero unless of course he is an absentee father or an overly abusive father, then he becomes an enemy rather than a hero in their eyes. As stated in the Holy Scripture, "Fathers, do not embitter your children, or they will become discouraged" (Colossians 4:14 NIV). The greatest praise a son can get is from his earthly father. Remember, every child wants to see their parents, particularly their fathers, as their heroes. The bottom line is that a father is a son's first hero and a daughter's first love.

The sixth letter and the second letter *A* in the acronym for fake fathers represents *absenteeism*. These, of course, are men who have little to nothing to do with their children's lives. I think it is important to understand that there are different degrees or levels of absenteeism. I say this because some men, even though they are physically in the home and around their children, have no real input in their child's life. Their children see them in the flesh but do not really know them. This type of man-child feels that if he is paying the bills, then that is the extent of his responsibilities as a father. As far as he is concerned, this is all his children need from him. Anything more than this, they can get it from their mother or other sources. This type of man-child and given the nature of the beast, I definitely have to call him a man-child, is in the same category as the man-child who simply pays his child support to the court every month with no thought of ever establishing a relationship with his children.

Then there is the man-child who just totally abandons his children or denies that they even exist. They make baby after baby with no regard for their children's health or well-being. It is truly unfortunate that far too many children find themselves in fatherless environments, based on absenteeism, to the point that it will profoundly impact the paths they take in their lives—paths that lead to selfishness, divorces, low self-esteem, and even a life of crime. Proverbs 27:8 (NIV) reminds us that "like a bird that strays from its nest is a man who strays from his home."

The seventh letter and the third letter *T* in the acronym for fake fathers represents the *taskmaster* man-child. This type of man-child can best be described as the man who bullies his children to maintain control of them. His mantra is, "There is only one way, and that's my way." In other words, his children must conform to his will irrespective of whether he is right or wrong. This type of man-child has a way of alienating his children with excessive discipline and control. For example, a former church member that I was once associated with demonstrated many of the traits of the taskmaster type. He had three sons, and he effectively alienated all three of them to the point that they not only became rebellious to his hard-core rule but also loss all respect for him. He caused this type of behavior in them by doing things like refusing to allow them to have any electronic devices; if he caught them with a device, he would confiscate and destroy them. In addition, since he had a military background, he ran his household like an army boot camp, and he was the drill sergeant. He showed his sons no patience or understanding if they did something wrong nor did he praise and show them any support when they did something right. It should go without saying that children need their father to feel pride in them, to tell them on a regular basis how much he loves them, and how proud he is of them, particularly in the case of the male child. Scripture warns us in Colossians 3:21 (NIV), "Parents don't come down too hard on your children or you'll crush their spirits."

The eighth letter and the fourth letter *H* in the acronym for fake fathers represents the *high and mighty* or headstrong man-child. This type of man-child is just an extension of the taskmaster type. They share similar traits in that they will never admit they are wrong. A headstrong man-child is so stuck on being right all the time even though the truth can be right in front of him, and he will still deny that it exists; such is the attitude of the atheist and the forty-fifth President of the United States, Donald J. Trump.

The ninth letter and the fifth letter *E* in the acronym for fake fathers represents the *egotistical* man-child. They can best be described as the man-child whose ego rules his life and is the driving force in how he raises his children. His ego will not allow him to change his flawed values and parenting paradigms that he may have learned from his father. In too many cases, these flawed values (as stated previously) are passed on from generation to generation. If one really thinks about it, you can easily see that this man-child trait is at the root of much of the racism, prejudice, and bias that we find in America today. In my opinion, a child is not born with these traits; they are all learned behaviors. Also, ego can be seen as an acronym that represents edging-God-out.

The tenth letter and sixth letter *R* in the acronym for fake fathers represents the *revolving-door* man-child. He is the type of man-child who pops in and out of his children's lives based on his own selfish needs rather than the needs of his children. His mantra can be summed up as, "When things go wrong, he gets gone." Just like a revolving door, he's in and out of his children's lives causing a completely unstable family environment, and, in too many cases, forcing his children to look elsewhere for stability. A good example of this trait can be seen in the popular TV show *Modern Family*. In multiple episodes, the young son (Manny) of one of the families is constantly being disappointed by his biological father who pops in and out of his life making promises he doesn't keep. For example, in one episode, he promised his son he was coming to see him and take him out on his new boat, but on the day he promised, the son waited and waited for his father who never showed up. Fortunately, his stepfather (Jay), who portrayed a real father figure, stepped in with an alternative plan to save the day from becoming a total disappointment.

In using the revolving door metaphor, one can easily relate to a door that just as quickly as it lets someone in, it just as quickly lets them out; it is constantly revolving in and out, and so it is with a man that is quickly there in their children's lives, and just as quickly, they are out of their lives. This type of man-child can be seen in men that are always on the road such as traveling salesman, truck drivers, business executives, and entertainers. They put their jobs and careers above the needs of their children. They think if they provide financial support and an occasional visit to the house, they have met their fatherly obligations. But their children get so used to their daddy being gone it becomes a way of life for them; in the final analysis, this man-child becomes, at best, nothing more than a stranger in his children's eyes.

The eleventh and final letter in fake father and the seventh letter *S* in the acronym fake fathers represents the *softies* man-child. This type of man-child can best be described as the man who is too weak and soft in nature to accept and step up to his fatherly responsibilities. Instead of stepping up to his duties as a father, he defers them to the mother of his children. He finds it easy and convenient to ignore the fact that his children need a father's protection, guidance, and nurturing love—things their mothers cannot give them. They need a father who is fully engaged, ready to take on the responsibilities of fatherhood, and to take on fully the leadership role of his family; let us be clear, a father is one of the most important images in the world of his child's life. A child relies on their fathers to answer the most critical questions in their lives. And the way a child's father tackles these questions can have a lasting effect on their lives.

If you can relate to any of the above traits, then this book is for you. I know I can, personally, because I have been involved in raising three children of my own. I can, unfortunately, relate to several of the above listed negative man-child traits. And, as I stated in the introduction, because I have made many of these mistakes, with regrettable consequences, it is one of the primary driving forces that has compelled me to write this book.

It is my firm belief that it is far better for a man to acknowledge his mistakes and move forward with a changed attitude than to continue on a course that will not only haunt him for the rest of his life but will also have devastating and lasting consequences on his children and family. It is my hope that by first exposing the negative traits of a fake father, I can provide insight as to what the building blocks of a real father looks like in the form of the seven pillars of fatherhood. And a real father, in my opinion, can be best summarized as a man that is *r*eliable, *e*ngaged, *a*vailable, and *l*oving.

Fatherhood Quiz

Question 1: Why is the presence of a godly father so important to the family unit?

Question 2: What is the core value of any society?

Question 3: Name and explain five negative traits of fake fathers?
1.
2.
3.
4.
5.

CHAPTER 2

Pillar 1—The Pilot Father

The most powerful leadership tool you have is your own personal example.

—John Wooden

The pilot pillar is the first of the foundational pillars. Unlike the last three pillars which constitute the maintenance pillars, this pillar—along with the "provide," "protect," and "prepare" pillars—constitute the foundational building blocks that all dedicated and committed real fathers must embrace in order that their children can have a solid start as they go through the growing and nurturing process.

The pilot-leader of a family must be strong and direct in his decision-making. He cannot waiver in his decision-making; for example, when we take a look at an aircraft pilot, we find that an aircraft pilot must be razor-sharp in his decision-making while taking off or landing an airplane all the while being vigilant throughout the flight because he knows he cannot afford to lose focus of the job at hand. Doing so would prove to be disastrous for all who are aboard his aircraft. In other words, this example emphasizes the fact that a good pilot-leader father must be on constant alert for possible and impending dangers that may affect the well-being and growth of his children and the well-being of his family. I think we have all seen in the news the devastating effects of a pilot who has lost his way in a storm and flies his plane into the side of a mountain or misjudged the takeoff or landing and crashes. So it is with a father pilot-leader of a family who gets caught up with the pitfalls and storms of life; these cause him to lose focus of the correct flight path and landing coordinates, so to speak, and instead directs his attention away from his family and children. He's now caught up in the pitfalls and storms of extramarital affairs, gambling, or other vices that keep him from honoring his fatherly responsibilities.

For a man to successfully raise his children, he must learn the ways of a good pilot-leader. Utilizing the example of a pilot of an aircraft again, he is entrusted with the safety and responsibility of his passengers; so it is with a father who must take on the role of leader of his family and children in terms of their safety, guidance, support, and spiritual awareness. And as the pilot-leader of his family, he must learn to lead his family in a way that gives his children a sense of positive direction—a sense of positive direction in the same way an airline pilot gives to his passengers when they board his aircraft. Just as a pilot has to safely take off and land a plane steering it away from dangerous obstacles, a real father has to navigate and steer his family and particularly his children away from the pitfalls and obstacles that we all face in a fallen world full of darkness and despair; these are pitfalls and obstacles that can impede the development of his children and keep them from becoming fruitful, productive men and women of God.

A good pilot-leader father must always be ready to make corrections when necessary. If the chosen path is leading him and his passengers (family) into a storm, he must be ready and able to change directions. For example, when his children are at an age that they are easily influenced by peer pressure and he has his family living in a neighborhood that is full of gang activities, then it would be prudent for him as the leader of his family to seek out another place to live. In other words, he must take his family in another direction away from possible and known hazards. Another example where a change of direction would be necessary is when the school district in the neighborhood is below par and not able to provide a solid foundational education for his children. As with the first example, it is up to the father as the pilot-leader of his family to find the best paths for his children's development, education, and nurturing. As stated previously, if he doesn't try and get his children out of a neighborhood that is full of crime, poor schools, and loaded with gang activities, then he shouldn't be surprised at the direction his children take in life. Or again, in the example of an airline pilot, don't be surprised when the aircraft he's piloting crashes and burns after going through a storm in an area he could have steered away from or, even worst, his passengers decided to bail out before he got them to the destination he was trying to get them to.

Speaking now from my own personal experience, after being blessed with my first of three children, a son, I found myself trying to find the best environment to raise him in; although, I didn't know, at the time, how critical this decision would be in his and my future first daughter's lives. I was twenty-four years old, fresh out of the military after serving my country for four years, and newly married. My focus at this time in my life was on affordable housing rather than suitable housing (in terms of a good neighborhood conducive to raising children), so I started out placing my family in an apartment in one of the rougher parts of the city I lived in; later, after my first daughter was born, I relocated them to a house in another rough area of the city. It was only after my son's first bike was stolen from him and my daughter started getting harassed and molested by some of the neighborhood kids that my wife and I decided it was time to make a move to a safer and more suitable neighborhood for raising our children. In my case, in retrospect, I made the move a little too late especially in terms of my son. And even though I subsequently moved my children to a better neighborhood, the damage was already done in terms of my son's path in life. You see, at this time in my son's life, he was at an age that he was dealing not only with raging hormones but also he was very impressionable and easily influenced by peer pressure. Let me be clear, I passionately believe that all fathers should bear in mind that a child without the guidance and direction of a fully engaged real father can be easily drawn into a lifestyle that will lead his children down a path of irreversible hurt, damage, and destruction.

DONALD H. WOOD, PH.D

After a lot of soul searching and reflection, I came to the realization that my past behavior can best be summed up in terms of a "fake father" as an absentee father. You see, at the time, not only was I singularly focused on just a better neighborhood but also I was too busy focusing on my selfish wants and desires such as job promotions and advancing my education rather than the well-being of my children and family. I didn't understand that children need more than a father image; they need the presence of a father. To put it another way, I lost sight as to what should have been most important in my life: being there for my children. I spent way too much time chasing after my personal wants and desires and all the while not realizing that my children and particularly my son was getting raised and influenced by the streets of Washington, DC.

One of the things I have learned about time is that you can't manage time; time manages you. You can either run with time, or time will run right past you. Time is limited and not reusable, and because of improper use of my time, my son subsequently became a pawn in the drug trafficking climate of the time in Washington, DC, which in the end caused him to lose his life way too soon at the age of twenty-one. Because of my absenteeism, my son found a substitute father figure in the form of a well-known drug kingpin. This drug kingpin taught him that it was all about the money, and if you want other people to look up, admire, and envy you, you had to be ruthless, lawless, and hedonistic. And even though my spouse and copilot, at the time, was deep into her Christian belief and tried desperately to point my son in the right direction, without the help and influence of me as his father, the battle was lost. I now realize that if I had been the type of real father that truly stepped up to his responsibilities as the pilot-leader of my family and not just leave the important aspects of raising my children to my copilot (wife), his life choices would have been completely different. What I needed to do at this critical time in his life was to spend as much time as I could with him so that he could imprint off of my best characteristics and not my worst. In addition, I should have been in a place in my life whereby I was able to guide and direct him in a godly direction; unfortunately, at this time in my life, I had never been personally taught nor had I ever accepted any godly direction. So it was not possible for me to give to him or pass on to him these critical characteristics that I now believe would have definitely impacted the course of his life. Statistically speaking, children brought up in homes with both parents that are believers in Christ have a far better chance of a loving and fulfilling childhood.

However, I did have a strong love for my children, a thirst for knowledge, good work ethics, and a sense of family, albeit not a correct sense of family which is one of the driving forces for me to write this book. Sadly, just as I was at that time in my life, there are far too many men, even in this day and age, struggling with how to be a successful father with not a clue as to why they are failing. They are failing as fathers, as did I, because they don't understand that fatherhood entails more than just one or two aspects or pillars of fatherhood but all seven pillars to be a real father and have a successful family. I say this because as I developed the seven pillars of fatherhood, I came to the realization that I was personally deficient in six of the seven pillars listed! The only pillar I really concentrated on and was successful in my fatherhood efforts was the "provide" pillar. I always made sure my children had food on the table, clothes on their backs, and a roof over their heads. To a certain extent, I was even a failure in this when you consider that I failed to understand that a father must be careful not to overprovide for his children. In retrospect, I think my overzealous need to provide for my children came as result of my own severe childhood poverty. In fact, I made myself a solemn promise when I was growing up that I would never let any children of mine suffer lack when it came to food, clothing, and shelter. Because as a child, I spend too many days hungry and wondering where my next meal would come from, not to mention the lack of proper clothing. In far too many occasions, it was a common practice for me and my siblings to look at food in a magazine and pretend we were eating it, more on this later. So it can easily be seen that because I came from a childhood that had a father that barely provided for his children, I learned how important it was to provide for my children. However, my personal experience has taught me a father must not substitute material possessions for quality time, patience, praise/

support, fatherly guidance, direct expressions of love, and heartfelt prayer; when it came to leading my family, I failed because a true pilot-leader is available and engaged and someone who can influence, inspire, and motivate others, especially his children.

In addition, I failed to protect my family because I let the evil influences of this world direct them instead of implementing my fatherly direction. I failed to prepare them (my children) to go forth into the world to be productive and fruitful citizens; especially in the case of my son, I failed to be patient when necessary and understanding as they went through the developmental stages of going from being a child to becoming an adult. I failed them because I did not praise and support, bolster, and build up their self-esteems. And finally, I failed them because unlike Job, as found in the Scriptures, I did not keep them raised up in prayer. Job understood that "perhaps my children have sinned and cursed God in their hearts" (Job 1:4–5 NIV). And, in far too many cases, with some children who become completely immersed in the sins of this world, prayers become a godly father's only go-to weapon to protect them.

As the pilot-leader of his family, a man must learn how to step up to the leadership position and guide and direct his family. And as the pilot of an aircraft, he is the one who must make all the critical decisions that will affect his family and ultimately guide and direct his children (the plane passengers) to their destinations and future. A true pilot-leader does not constantly rely on his copilot (wife) for the task that is better suited for him and not her. This is not to say that a copilot (wife) cannot do the job of the pilot, which has been proven throughout history that she can and is more than able when placed in the position to lead the family. However, the best situation is to have the pilot (father) as the head of the family backed up by his helpmate copilot (wife). As stated previously, in terms of a man's children, their father is the most powerful man in their world; in the words of John Eldredge in his book *You Have What It Takes*, "Your children are looking to you to answer the deepest questions of their lives. How you handle their hearts will shape them for the rest of their lives." And because a child sees their father in such a powerful way, some things must be taught to a child by their father (or father figure) and not their mother. For example, in the case of the male and female child, again according John Eldredge, the male child learns if he has what it takes to be a man from his father; in the case of the female child, she learns from her father that she is worth pursuing and that she is beautiful. Personally, as a father of two daughters, I always try to remember how important my love and attention is to them. Although they are both grown women now, I still try to keep a close, loving, and bonding relationships with them. Because they are no longer children, the maintenance pillars that include patience, praising, and praying are my go-to pillars to enhance and maintain my relationship with them. To emphasize why it's so important for a father to be the first and most important man in his son and daughter's lives, we find in Steven Covey's book *The 7 Habits of Highly Effective Families* where he stressed the fact that a good father should set aside time just for his daughter or son at least once a month or so. So if you are reading this book and you are a father, you should be asking yourself, *Am I setting aside quality time just for my children?*

As I have stated before, personally, I am the father of two daughters who I am extremely proud of and love dearly. Even though they are grown now, as I look back and have stated previously, I know now that while I was raising them, I fell short in several of the pillars of fatherhood. I say this because, again as I have stated previously, although I was a good provider and excellent protector, I fell short when it came to being a pilot-leader, preparer, supporter, practicing patience when necessary, and praying for my children. Let me be completely clear, I fell short in these areas because, at the time of their child-rearing, I had no concept of how important it was for me as their father to prepare them for life's ups and downs, to praise and support them when they most needed it, to be patient as they faced the challenges of peer pressure, hormonal changes, and finally to go to my Lord and Savior in prayer when all else failed. Unfortunately, in the case of my only begotten son whom I lost when he was only twenty-one, I fell not just short of the mark but was a total failure; as a consequence, I continue to suffer one of the worst things any parent can face: the loss of a child. You see, something I can't emphasize enough at the time of his loss, I was more focused on me and not my family. I really didn't have any real concept of how to be a good father, much less a pilot-leader of a family. I did not realize, particularly in the case of a male child, that to be a good father or even more so a real father, I had to be more than just the guy that paid the bills.

The first example in my life in terms of what the head of a household looked like was my biological father who I only knew from afar because I never lived in the same house with him until my high school years. My other examples are my older brothers and my atheist brother-in-law who were not much better as father figures. Unfortunately, by the time I did move in with my biological father, the mold was set, so to speak; my concept of fatherhood was largely based on what I gleaned from my older brothers and my atheist brother-in-law. And because I spent most of my younger years with my sister and her husband (the atheist), I didn't learn any real pilot-leadership values even though I was placed in a family which, on the surface, appeared to be a stable atmosphere—an atmosphere which I quickly discovered was toxic. You see, I lost my mother at the age of nine, and instead of stepping up to the plate and taking charge of the family—which by this time consisted of seven daughters and five sons with seven of the twelve grown adults—my father made the choice to place the younger five children in the care of the older siblings. So as it turned out, I was bounced from one older sister to the next until, by the time I reached my junior high school years, I wound up with my devout Roman Catholic older sister and her atheist husband who, by this time, already had seven mouths to feed of their own.

As a father figure and pilot-leader, my brother-in-law from a positive standpoint, could be described as a man that worked hard and provided for family. This was a man who worked two jobs: a mailman during the day and a cab driver at night. However, from a negative standpoint, he drank alcohol excessively, didn't believe in God, was physically and verbally abusive to my sister, and had a weird sense of manhood. His concept of manhood was that the provider of the house was supposed to be a dictator and a taskmaster. I can recall on more than one occasion when he talked about his military days spent in Korea. He admired the fact that Korean women were so subservient to their husbands; they would always walk four feet behind him just off his left shoulder, and they would speak only when spoken to. Given this misogynist view and so many other chauvinistic ideas about marriage and family, it's not hard to understand why he had no concept of what it took to be a true pilot-leader of a family.

Throughout the time I spent under his roof, he would constantly challenge my fragile young male ego by saying things like, "You're weak, and you'll never become a real man" and otherwise attack my frail self-esteem. He never supported any of my dreams nor did he ever spend any quality time with me. Fortunately, instead of letting this kind of negative atmosphere affect how I viewed life, I became determined to prove him wrong. Finally, things got so bad with this living situation (living with my sister and her husband), and after I came to the realization that I was just another mouth to feed, I left my sister's house and luckily was taken in by my father and his second wife. The takeaway from the experience I had in my brother-in-law's household can best be described by a quote by Dean Koontz: "There's sometimes a weird benefit to having an alcoholic violent father." To put it simply, my experience with my brother-in-law really motivated me to not be anything like him. And so it was with the time I spent with my sister and her husband that I came to realize that he taught me exactly the type of fatherhood behaviors that are contrary to a positive pilot-leader of a family.

My time with my biological father were not the best of times either, especially in terms of the seven pillars fatherhood. Although I finally was in a family setting where I felt safe, provided for, and my self-esteem didn't come under daily attack, I still never felt my father was a true pilot-leader or head of his household. I say this because unlike my brother-in-law who was an overbearing chauvinist, my father was docile and let my stepmother and her sister rule the household. In addition, he spent no real quality time with me. He never took me to a baseball game (and he was avid baseball fan), football, or basketball game. In fact, even though I played high school football, he never attended one of my games. In addition, it's amazing to me how—even after all these years that I've been on God's green earth and although my father has long since gone home to be with the Lord—I cannot remember a time when he actually spoke to me verbally that he loved me or that he was proud of me. Don't get me wrong, although he didn't say the words out of his mouth, I knew deep down he did love me and was proud of me because of his actions. But a child, and particularly a male child, should never be left wondering if their father loves them, especially in their formative years. It's also important to note that a big part of a child's life is their parent's approval, which all relates to the praising pillar which I will discuss in-depth in chapter 6. This early validation helps to boost a young child's self-esteem and foster a deep sense of security that can only come from their parents especially their father. For the life of me, as with my father, I will never understand why some men think it's okay to express love verbally to their daughters but have a problem with expressing love verbally to their sons. This kind of double standard was also validated by my fatherhood survey results. Too many men have this hidden macho code that says that if I show physical love for my son, somehow, this will make him into a sissy. Of course, nothing could be further from the truth.

The bottom line is this: as a father, it is imperative that if he want to be a successful pilot-leader of his family, he must be first and foremost available. Second, he must learn to stay engage with his children, which requires that he works and plays with his children at every opportunity. This is especially important in a child's early years to the extent that some researchers say that focusing on play behavior is essential to fathering a child just as nurturing behavior is essential to mothering. This means that if a father's little girl wants to have a tea party with him, he shouldn't just brush her off; he should sit down and have a tea party with her. If his son wants his father to play video games with him, his father should take the time out of his day and play video games, and he should never overlook the chance to tuck in and read his son or daughter bedtime stories. One of things I got in the habit of doing with my girls when they were growing up was to take them to school or drive them to the bus stop and wait for the school bus with them. This gave me the opportunity to interact, bond, and engage in conversation and pray with them. Trust me, these simple little acts of love that involve availability, engagement, and quality time will have an everlasting effect on them. Finally, a real father must lead by example. A strong father example in the areas of their spiritual, physical, nutritional, social, emotional, financial, and intellectual endeavors will have a strong influence in the development of moral standards, positive values, and confidence in a son or daughter. Remember, fathers or father figures are the greatest hero in a child's life, and they will imprint and learn what is good or bad from watching their father. So if their father drinks excessively and it's his regular habit to come home drunk, it should come as no surprise when his child decides to do the same. The same can be said about smoking, overeating, foul language, lack of educational effort, being a social pariah, and being spiritually disconnected. In other words, if fathers don't practice what they preach, their children will ignore their advice and instead imprint from their example. And in the words of Charles Kettering, "Every father should remember that one day his son will follow his example rather than his advice."

Let me end this chapter with a few words of wisdom from the Father of all fathers, our Creator, who reminds us that "the righteous lead blameless lives blessed are their children after them (Proverbs 20:7 NIV). So all fathers and future fathers must ask themselves, Am I ready to lead a blameless life for the sake of my children?

Fatherhood Quiz

Question 1: What are some of the characteristic of a good pilot-leader?

Question 2: Why is it important for a father to set aside quality time to spend with his children?

Question 3: Why is it important that a father express love to his son and daughter equally, both verbally and nonverbally?

Question 4: If a man wants to be a successful pilot-leader of his family, he must focus on what three things?

Question 5: Why is it important to lead not just by words but also by example?

CHAPTER 3

Pillar 2—The Provider Father

If anyone does not provide for his relatives, and especially for his immediate family, he has denied the faith and is worse than an unbeliever.
—1 Timothy 5:8 (NIV)

There is a popular TV show hosted by Maury Povich that deals almost exclusively with paternity testing, and one of the first questions the host always ask a potential father before he reveals a DNA test is, "If you are the father you will step up and provide for and be in this child's life, won't you?" You may think, obviously, the answer to this question should be a resounding yes. However, this is an extremely important question given the current trend in the number of children that have been abandoned by their biological fathers. Statistically speaking, the cost of raising a child in the United States from infancy to the age of eighteen is $233,610, and there are 8.5 million single women in the United States raising children without the benefit of their child's father. In addition, a staggering 2.5 million children are now homeless each year in America. This represents a historical high of one in every thirty children that are homeless. An estimated 24.7 million children (33 percent) live with their absentee biological fathers. Of students in grades 1 through 12, 39 percent (17.7 million) live in homes with their absentee biological fathers, 57.6 percent of black children, 20.7 percent of Hispanic children, and 20.7 percent of white children are living with their absentee biological fathers. And according to 72.2 percent of the US population, fatherlessness is the most significant family or social problem facing America. These are alarming statistics that all point to the fact that there are far too many "baby daddy situations" which means children are not being properly provided for either financially or otherwise.

The provider pillar is the second of the foundational pillars and is not only one of the most important pillars financially but also one of the most misunderstood. I say this because, in too many cases, men have the distorted idea that all they need to do is provide food, clothing, and shelter for their children, then they have met their fatherly obligations. As a father, they don't understand that they must provide more than just food, clothing, and shelter. You must also provide an atmosphere of love and caring for both the female as well as the male child. It's interesting to note this concept of showing love and affection for the male child is contrary to most men's upbringing. They think if they show love and affection to their sons, somehow, that will make them into a sissy and a weak man. Nothing is further from the truth. A son needs his father's hugs and affection just as much as his sister. In far too many cases, the male child sees their father showing love and affection for his mother and his sister(s) and wonders why doesn't he show him this type of love? He may even ask himself if he did something wrong.

Speaking now from my own childhood experience from a provider's perspective, my experience with my biological father, as stated previously, can best be described as him being an absentee father. This, of course, describes a man who although he provides some financial support to his children and family but otherwise has nothing to do with his children's day-to-day child-rearing.

Again, speaking from my own childhood experience, life began in an atmosphere of poverty. I was born into a family that consisted of five boys and seven girls. I came along as part of the second set of six children. I am the youngest brother in my family, and by the time I came along, my parents had decided to part ways; my father moved out the house and took up residence in another section of the city we lived in. He left my mother with the task of raising the second set of children on her own, who at this time were still underage, in a poverty-stricken housing development in the northeast section of Washington, DC. To make things worse, after my father's departure, my mother's health began to quickly deteriorate; she passed away in the ninth year of my life at the age of forty-seven of a massive cerebral hemorrhage (stroke).

Because of my father's absenteeism negatively impacting the first nine years of my life and before my mother's passing, my life consisted of basic survival: food, clothing, and shelter. Things got so bad at this time in my life that in order to survive, it was a regular practice, in an effort to find food to eat, to go the local landfill/dump and forage through the trash and garbage for edible food. And there were far too many days when food became so scarce my siblings and I would eat sugar and butter sandwiches or, on many other occasions, just sandwiches made from grease. And when things really got bad (as if things were not bad enough), we were only left with our imagination. In other words, as I stated previously, we would find a magazine that had pictures of delicious food we wish we had and imagine we were eating the same. Because of the poverty and neglect, we were also deprived of other basic comforts that others take for granted. In the winter months, we were never fortunate enough to have enough heat because my mother never had enough money to purchase coal for the coal-burning furnace in our house. This was the type of heating fuel that was in use during my childhood. So to stay warm, we (my siblings and I) would get in a bed together and cover ourselves up with blankets and coats to stay warm through cold winter nights. And in the hot steamy summer months, there was no such thing as an air conditioner or fans, we would simply open all the windows in the house or slept on the front porch in hopes of catching a cool summer nighttime breeze. This neglect also had a profound effect on my educational development as well. These educational development setbacks included being placed in school at the age of eight with things getting progressively worse because of the lack of proper clothing; this meant I had to go to school with holes in my socks and shoes and without a warm coat to wear. Then when you factor in an empty growling belly, it should come as no surprise that this ongoing neglect played a major part in the fact that I wound up repeating the third grade. When you are forced into a survival mode no matter how young you are, school and all that it represents is the last thing that's on your young mind. This focus on survival rather than school, of course, now meant I found myself not just one but two years behind in my formal educational development. Because of my father's lack of properly providing and absenteeism, my neglect was so pervasive that at some point in my early childhood, I dislocated my collar bone; this was ignored and not afforded any medical attention to the point that to this day, I live with a fused right collar bone. This neglect also extended to my lack of dental care as well. Because by the time I joined the United States Air Force, half of my teeth were cavity-ridden.

At this point, let me make it clear that I loved my father despite of his shortcomings when it came to him providing for me during some of the key developmental years of my life. I now realize he gave the best he was capable and able to provide for me at that time in his life. He was operating with an eighth-grade education; his own father, a window washer, died early in his life falling from a highrise building to his death. After his father's death, he found himself having to basically raise himself. And then after marrying my mother who was only fourteen at the time of their marriage, he quickly found himself having to raise and support twelve children. This brings me to an important point in terms of the subject of providing. Every man and potential father should always remember that you should not bring a child into this world if you cannot properly provide for them. And in the words of the late Episcopal Pastor John A. Cherry, "there is no such thing as an illegitimate child, only an illegitimate parent," particularly if you have overextended yourself by having multiple children or have limited resources. In other words, if you cannot afford them (children), think twice, even three times, before you make them! To make matters worse, too many men overextend themselves by having not only multiple children but also multiple women. As pointed out from the statistics in the beginning of this chapter, if it's expensive to raise just one child, then just think what it cost to raise multiple children while dealing with multiple women. It's really sad to note that, in far too many cases, when a man overextends himself in situations like this, the child suffers. It's not fair to a child to be brought into an environment of poverty and despair all because a man could not control his flesh. All children—and I repeat, all children—deserve to be raised in a loving, nurturing home environment.

In addition, in my father's case, he was what I can further describe as a short distance absentee provider. I say this because although he didn't live in the house with us, he did reside in the same city that my siblings and I lived in. This, of course, is not always the case. For example, I have a neighbor who moved into the neighborhood I currently live in with his wife and three children about twenty years ago. Within those twenty years, around year ten, I watched him move out of his home leaving his three children to be raised by their mother while he supposedly sought employment in a distant state. He rarely comes to visit his children, and over the years, I have noticed the effects of how his neglect and absenteeism has played a role in his children's development. His oldest daughter is currently living with a man out of wedlock; his youngest daughter is still living in the home with her mother with all sorts of psychological issues, and his son is also still living with his mother although he's now twenty-five years old while spending his days playing video games. Their father's lack of providing for his family over the years can be seen not only in the way his children are currently living their lives but also from the fact that the home they live in is in constant disrepair; the utilities are constantly being turned off for lack of payment. In addition, you can see the toll it has taken on his wife having to raise three children during some of the most critical developmental years of her children's lives without the help of their father. This all points to how impactful a father's role are to the family unit. In fact, children with absentee fathers are

- four times at greater risk of poverty,
- seven times more likely to become pregnant as a teen,
- more likely to have behavioral problems,

- two times at greater risk of infant mortality,
- more likely to commit a crime,
- more likely to face abuse and neglect,
- more likely to abuse drugs and alcohol,
- two times more likely to suffer obesity, and
- two times more likely to drop out of high school.

Remember, in terms of the family unit, the best family dynamic includes both a father and a mother or, as I like to say, a pilot and copilot. The two work best as a team, and just as in the case of a pilot and copilot in the example of an aircraft, the copilot is the backup for the pilot, but the pilot is, first and foremost, in charge of the aircraft. And so it is with a family unit; the best family dynamic is to have a strong father or father figure as the head of the family with a strong woman as his team member and backup.

The bottom line is this: it is imperative that every man that is blessed with the opportunity to raise children come to the realization that it takes more than just financial assistance or just cursory interaction with their children from time to time to truly raise stable and productive children. Children need a father's love and attention just as much as they need their mother's. It's not enough just to be known as a "baby's daddy." A strong father presence, engagement, and attention is vitally important in the development of a son or daughter's identity, values, morals, and confidence.

Far too many men think all they need to do is "bring home the bacon," and that is the extent of their involvement with their children. They have a mistaken belief that certain tasks like taking their children to doctor's appointments, day care, after school activities, etc. are the exclusive duties of their copilot (wives). This disengagement with their children is so pervasive to the extent that when they are, for example, forced to take the children to a doctor's appointment and the doctor ask them something about their children's medical history, in far too many cases, they don't know their children's ages, birthdays, or even what their children are allergic to. This was driven home in a current popular reality TV show called *Love & Marriage: Huntsville*. One of the couples featured on the show have three young children who, on one episode, are left in the care of their father for a day because their mother had decided it was time for her to return to the workplace. Their father who has had nothing to do with their early childhood nurturing and had been disengaged with them except for "bringing home the bacon" now finds himself feeling like a fish out of water. In fact, when he attempts to fix them a meal and they object to what he's cooking, he tells them to go and fix themselves peanut butter and jelly sandwiches; one of his sons responds, "But, Daddy, don't you know I'm allergic to peanuts?" This is a father who is more concerned with his job and making money to the point that his children are placed on the back burner when it comes to his attention. In other words, he's a man who truly feels that the raising and nurturing of children is a woman's job.

As I conclude this chapter, let me leave you with seven key points every real father should embrace:

Point number 1. Always remember that providing financially for your children is a basic responsibility that all real fathers embrace without question. It is unconscionable to think that providing food, shelter, and clothing for your children is somehow the responsibility of their mother, grandparents, or the government.

Point number 2. Always remember that providing for your children is a basic responsibility, but it is also extremely important to provide your children with time and attention. Too many fathers think that all they must do is simply "bring home the bacon," and that is the extent of their responsibility. This is a myth, and nothing could be further from the truth.

Point number 3. Always remember that your children want your love and attention. Don't ever be afraid to tell your children you love them. Unfortunately, too often in our current culture, many men have this misguided idea that a man should not tell and express his love for his children, especially his sons. To do so would make them less of a man because this kind of sentimentally is something reserved only for women.

Point number 4. Always remember that you never stop providing for your children even after they become adults. As a father, you still need to provide them with love, support, and prayer. It should also be noted a father must be careful not to overprovide for his children. In other words, he must not substitute materials possessions for quality time.

Point number 5. Always remember your children are always seeking your approval. It doesn't matter if you are married to their mother or otherwise estranged from them. No matter what the situation, deep down, they still want you to be pleased with them.

Point number 6. Always remember you are a king in your children's eyes. And as their king, they import their values and morals from you. If their king, for example, smokes, drinks excessively, gambles, womanizes, and fails to provide properly for his children, then there is an exceptionally good chance his children will follow in his footsteps. In contrast, if their king is a God-fearing, family-centered, nonsmoker, nondrinker, nongambler, then, of course, the chances are his children will adapt these same morals and values. I can safely state this because of my own experience with the three children I help to bring into this world. Because I never smoked, gambled, or drank alcohol in excess, they too never adopted any of these bad habits. Unfortunately, in contrast, in my son's case, he imprinted on many of my bad values and lack of moral scruples that I had imprinted from my father and the father figures in my life during my childhood.

Point number 7. Finally, and it bears repeating, always remember—as a wise man once taught me—there is no such thing as illegitimate children, only illegitimate parents. So when it comes to stepping up to the plate and providing for the children you bring into this world, you must ask yourself this question, Am I an illegitimate father, and if I am, am I willing to step up and be the legitimate real father God intended me to be?

THE SEVEN PILLARS OF FATHERHOOD

Fatherhood Quiz

1. Statistically speaking, what does it cost to raise a child in the United States from infancy to age eighteen?

2. Approximately, how many children live in homes without their biological fathers?

3. What are three key points (seven were given) that all fathers should remember when it comes to providing for their children?
   a.
   b.
   c.

CHAPTER 4

Pillar 3—The Protector Father

I cannot think of a need in childhood as strong as the need for a father's protection.
—Sigmund Freud

Nothing is more shocking than to turn on the local news and hear that another young child was killed by a stray bullet or hear an Amber Alert announcing that another child has been abducted by some perverted predator. This kind of news has unfortunately become far too much the norm rather than the exception and points to an even greater need for all fathers to step up and protect their children.

All real fathers know how to protect their families from the predators of life; in the current climate of the times, the child molesters, bullies, and rapist are now running rampant. A real father must also protect his children's minds from the constant bombardment of ungodly media decadence that is so prevalent today, always remembering the old quote "Garbage in, garbage out." In addition, a real father must protect his children from all real and potential disasters arising from inexperience and impulsive mistakes (especially in their early childhood); examples including but not limited to playing with matches, grabbing hot objects, drinking poisonous substances, and making sure they are fastened safely in their car seats or seats belts whenever they are in a vehicle. So it can be seen from these examples, and as you will find later in this chapter, that a father's protection starts at the conception of their children and lasts throughout their lives.

It is also interesting to note that the protect instinct tends to be something that is innate in most, if not all, men. God seems to have empowered men with the physical and mental strength they need to protect those that they love. This instinct lies in the very core of every God-fearing man's masculinity and is a force to reckon with once released. If you don't believe this is so, just watch how fast a man goes into action to protect his daughter from potential suitors or when someone disrespects his wife or significant other.

Just recently, I watched on the nightly news a shooting incident in a car dealership in which three gunmen started spraying bullets in the showroom where a father was sitting on a sofa with his three small children. Sensing danger, the father immediately grabbed all three of his young children and fell on the floor with them and quickly covered them under his body. Because of his quick actions, his children were unharmed, but unfortunately, he was struck by one of the stray bullets in his upper thigh but survived.

Pillar 3, the protector father is the third foundational pillar which makes up the third of the four foundational pillars. And as Sigmund Freud had noted, there is no other need as strong as this in a child's life.

Every father must learn to protect his children from the powers and evil of what I like to call PET. It's an acronym that represents the following:

P—peer pressure and predators. Peer pressure is something too many children face in today's current climate of the times. Also, in far too many cases, the damage is done before most parents become aware of the situation and in worst-case scenarios can cause their children to commit suicide or cause them to otherwise harm themselves. To emphasize this point, let me share with you an incident that involved one of my neighbor's sons. On one quiet summer afternoon, as I was returning from a dental appointment with my wife, she noticed that one of our neighbor's son was joyriding through the neighborhood with a group of other neighborhood kids. This was not only strange but also sent up all kinds of red flags because he was underage and so were his passengers. Once we notified his parents, we realized that he did not have permission from his parents to drive the vehicle he was in, much less to joyride a rather expensive SUV through the neighborhood with his underage peer group. It was obvious to us that he was being influenced by his passengers, his peer group, who edged him on. Fortunately, we chased him down and finally cornered him at the end of a cul-de-sac in our neighborhood and took the keys away from him. This could have ended tragically if my wife and I had not intervened. His peer group of passengers could have edged him on right into a serious accident, especially given the fact that he was an inexperienced, unlicensed, underage driver. Remember, just because your children tell you they won't do something doesn't mean they are going to keep their word. Peer pressure can make them lose all sense of right or wrong. And I, for one, can testify to the fact that raging hormones are real, and they can make your kids seem to lose their minds and do all kinds of dumb stuff!

In addition, as stated previously, this world is, unfortunately, full of predators just waiting to abuse and corrupt our children. They can be found in the malls, hanging around your children's school, maybe even working at your children's school, and trolling on online websites pretending to be a naive child's friend. Again, let me share an incident that my wife and I experienced with our youngest daughter when she was thirteen years old. This incidence occurred during her summer break from school when, out of the blue, one day, she asked my wife to drop her and one of her girlfriends off at our local mall. Fortunately, my wife was suspicious but didn't take the request too seriously until she got a call from one of her nieces who noticed on an internet social media site that our daughter was communicating on, what turned out to be a sexual predator she met online who was trolling the internet. After getting over the initial shock, we shut the situation down immediately and had a long conversation with our daughter who said she was bored, and she didn't see any harm in talking to someone she met on the internet who simply wanted to be her friend. Remember, she was only thirteen at the time and very impressionable. Although I got involved along with my wife as soon as we became aware of the situation, it would have never happened in the first place had I, as her father, been on my job as her protector. I say this because at the time, I was working a full-time job and two part time jobs, all of which kept me from spending enough quality time with my daughter. Remember, you must raise your children, and in this case a daughter, to always trust your judgment when it comes to the issues of life. If you gain their trust at an early age, you will be their anchor as they cope with life's ups and downs, and they will never feel the need to turn to strangers on the internet or anyplace else.

I had another incidence with my other older daughter that occurred when she was in her second year of high school. She came home one day and told me she was being harassed by a pizza shop worker who worked near the subway station she walked by every day after school en route to coming home. In this case, my innate fatherly instincts immediately kicked in, and I confronted this predator and threatened him with bodily harm if he didn't stop harassing my child. The message was received, and the problem was solved.

I would be remiss if I did not address the drug dealer predators that are constantly trying to entice our children into a life of drug abuse and crime. This, unfortunately, was the reason why I personally lost my only begotten son, which to this day hurts me to the core of my soul. He lost his life after being shot to death on the streets of Washington, DC, at the age of twenty-one. I passionately believed that his untimely death was due in part to my lack of basic fatherly skills such as the seven "Ps" of fatherhood and the fact that he was heavily influenced and enticed into illicit drug dealing by a drug-dealing kingpin (the ultimate predator) that was in operation in Washington, DC, at the time of his death. This drug dealing kingpin, like all drug dealing kingpins, enticed my raging hormones, immature son with the illusion of fast money and the unrealistic need for immediate gratification. I can go on with these examples, but suffice it to say, this problem hasn't gotten any better; even though this took place over twenty-five years ago, it is still out of control with today's young people.

E—represents the environment and all its negative influences found in social media, etc. It's up to all real fathers to guard their children's minds from the constant bombardment of toxic music, movies, videos, people, and language they are subjected to on a daily basis. This is not an easy thing to do, but it is something that is vitally important if you want your children to develop proper morals and values patterned after you and not what they encounter in the streets, social media, and the world.

T—represents themselves or their self-image which is directly influenced by peer pressure, predators, and the environment. A child's teenage years are a critical time in their lives because they are trying to decide who they are spiritually, sexually, socially, and personally. Spiritually speaking, if your children don't accept the truth of who they are in Jesus Christ, they will be subjected to what the world likes to call "finding my own truth." Make no mistake about it, there is only one truth that really counts, and that's God's truth. Sexually speaking, if they follow the ways of the world, they will be constantly operating in a state of contradiction. Socially speaking, without a real father's guidance, they will be slaves to social media and utilize as their role models all of the so-called entertainers and celebrities on how to relate to others. And finally, speaking personally, they will be left to emulate decadent people they find on social media and within their peer group.

All father's must make PET their pet project, so to speak, in their children's lives in order to properly protect them in this fallen world full of darkness and despair.

All though I focused a lot on the latter and formative years of father's and children's lives, it is also important that all real fathers be on guard for their children's protection when they are in the womb, newborn, or toddlers. All real fathers recognize that it is their responsibility, just as much as their mate's, to make sure that their children have the best possible chance for a healthy beginning in this life, and it all starts with proper prenatal care. A real father must make sure that his baby's mother is protected in every way possible from anything that could injure her and his unborn child. This includes alcohol, smoking, improper or nutritional empty food, falls, stress, and driving hazards. Once a baby is born, a father must protect them with safeguards to prevent injuries from falls and accident by putting up staircase guards, cabinet safety locks, proper car seats, and baby carriers. It is also important that he be on guard for sudden infant death syndrome (SIDS), otherwise known as crib death. He has to make sure, as his children's number one protector, that when they are infants, they sleep on their backs in their cribs and always monitor their sleep with a baby monitor. It bears repeating that these things, as outlined, are not just the responsibility of his children's mother but him as well. To emphasize this point, let me point to a study conducted in 2016 by Michigan State University that found a father's relationship with their children from toddler through to fifth grade was important in their children's health and development.

Finally, it's vitally important that all real fathers protect their children by strengthening them both emotionally and mentally; that way, they can later protect themselves and later their own families based on your loving protective leadership that guided them into becoming responsible, competent adults. This leads me into the next pillar which involves a father's role in preparing his children to leave the nest.

DONALD H. WOOD, PH.D

Fatherhood Quiz

1. Other than a father protecting his children from bodily harm, what else must he protect them from?

2. What does the acronym PET represent?

3. In terms of predators and children, who's seen as one of the ultimate predators?

4. Why is it important that a father be on guard for his children's safety when they are in the womb, newborn, or toddlers?

5. What does the acronym SID represent?

CHAPTER 5

Pillar 4—The Preparing Father

If you give a man a fish you feed him for a day, but if you teach him how to fish, you feed him for a lifetime.
—Chinese Proverb

Have you ever noticed the number of grown children still living at home? I'm talking about folks that are, in many cases, in their late twenties and sometimes in their thirties. This phenomenon is well known as the boomerang effect, and it points to the fact that a lot of fathers failed to prepare their children to leave the (nest) home. Just like a bird kicks his baby birds out of the nest when they are ready to fly, it is the responsibility of all real fathers to do the same for his children; otherwise, they will never learn how to live on their own, and they will continue to be dependent people rather than learning how to be independent people.

To start our discussion on pillar 4, we must stress the fact that all real fathers recognize how important it is to start the foundational or mentoring preparatory process early in their children's lives; it must start with him singing, talking, and reading to his children daily. As an established mentor, he will be seen in his children's eyes as the person who provides them with guidance, motivation, inspiration, emotional support, and fatherly advice.

In addition, once these basic foundational or mentoring behaviors are well-established between a father and his children, a real father knows that he must prepare and teach his children how to be self-sufficient and independent in preparation for the day when they will have to leave the nest. There is something that can be said about the old Chinese proverb that says, "If you give a man a fish you feed him for a day but if you teach him how to fish you feed him for a lifetime." This proverb emphasizes the point that its far better to prepare and teach your children how to take care of themselves rather than them always depending on Mommy and Daddy for the rest of their lives. If we look closely at the definition for the word *prepare*, we find it is defined as to "make ready beforehand for some purpose, use, or activity and to put in a proper state of mind." Given these definitions, a father must make sure that his children are ready beforehand to face life challenges and that they are in their proper state of mind when it comes to their spiritual, physical, nutritional, social, emotional, intellectual, and financial endeavors in life.

If children are not prepared to go forth in life, as I stated in the chapter introduction, you'll find that far too many children stay under their parents' roof for far too long after they finish school. I'm not just talking about high school but even college. Remember, too many parents make it too easy for their children to simply never move out of the house and learn how to be responsible for themselves. This type of situation, in many cases, is derived from the fact that many mothers do not want to see their babies grow up and are reluctant to see them move from under their care. They reason, after all, the world is full of all kinds of predators, dangers, and it's part of her motherly instincts to protect her babies; the best way to do this is to keep them close to her, under her roof and care. However, as a father with an eye to prepare his children to leave the nest to become productive, independent, fruitful, and responsible adults, he must step forward and kick them out of the nest so that they can fly, so to speak, on their own. And if they are not kicked out of the nest, they will never learn how to fly on their own. But before he kicks them out of the nest, he must prepare them in seven vital areas of responsibilities: spiritual, physical, nutritional, social, emotional, financial, and intellectual. In other words, as a real father, he must prepare and teach his children to go forth ready to take on the world spiritually, nutritionally, socially, emotionally, intellectually, and financially.

In the area of the spirituality, it is his responsibility, as a father, to make sure his children are introduced to their Creator. Remember, we come to Christ our Lord and savior through revelation, not explanation, and the best way a father can reveal Christ to his children is through their example: by openly praying with them, regular church attendance, and by teaching them how to pray on their own. I personally made it a practice to pray with my youngest daughter while we waited for her school bus. It bears repeating that fathers are their children's first and foremost example. If a father ignores the Lord, then it should come as no surprise that their children will develop a spiritual disconnect with their Creator. And we find in Proverbs 4:1–4 (NIV) an admonishment from the Creator which states, "Listen, my sons, to a father's instruction, pay attention and gain understanding. I give you sound learning so do not forsake my teaching. For I too was a son to my father, still tender, and cherished by my mother. Then he taught me, and he said to me, take hold of my words with all your heart; keep my commands, and you will live."

A life not based on a sound spiritual foundation is a life doomed to failure. True prosperity is not about money and fame but about finding favor with man and God. Life is not about finding temporary happiness through fame and fortune but through a spiritual connection that affords us with a chance for a life of peace, joy, and hope. You noticed that I stated happiness is temporary; it comes and goes like the wind and is dependent on what's going on around you at a given time. Whereas peace, joy, and hope are things that are dependent on what's going on inside of you and can only come from a vertical heavenly source, not a horizontal environmental source like happiness.

When I reflect on my own personal experience, one of the things I most regret in life is the fact that it took me fifty years to develop a relationship with my Lord and Savior and a spiritual foundation. You see, I was never taught nor did I have any good examples of what a spirit-filled, godly man was or should look or act like. My only examples were, as I have stated previously, an absentee biological father, my older brothers, and an atheist brother-in-law. All of whom were men that had either a total distaste for the church and anything remotely spiritual or just didn't put any emphasis on the church or their Creator. For the most part, my examples believed church was something women embraced and that all church leaders were no more than "pimps in the pulpit" in the business of using the church to make money by fleecing the flock out of as much money as they could. This attitude was reinforced by the fact that there was a church on every corner, yet I saw no real evidence of godly love and obedience in the people that came out of their doors.

What many men do not understand is how important a child's spiritual foundation is until it is too late. A child must be taught right from wrong, and it all starts with childhood rearing. If you don't teach and show your children correct behavior and, more importantly, help them in their spiritual development that will heighten their sense of conscience, they won't be prepared to face life's temptations as they go forth into a fallen world full of darkness and despair.

I think it should be clear by now that when it comes to preparing your children spiritually, it's not just their mother's responsibility but even more so a father's as their children's number one role model. This is even more important in the case of male children. Remember if a child's father doesn't take the Creator seriously and makes no effort to build a spiritual foundation and relationship with the Creator, then he should not expect his children to do anything different.

The next area of responsibility a father must prepare his children for is how to properly take care of themselves physically. In far too many cases, we see young kids with no concept of physical fitness or proper hygiene. These things must be taught and modeled by their fathers or father figures. They are not just things a kid teaches themselves or something that should be left to their mothers to teach them. Or even worst, without the guidance of a real father, children are left to pick up these things from social media or the streets. For example, a son will watch his father shave in the morning, and even though he hasn't grown a beard yet, he will still try to copy his father's behavior. In this case, he learns from his daddy that a well-shaved man is a man who cares about his appearance. In contrast, if he sees that his father or father figure who never shaves and wears an unkempt scraggly beard and this is what he sees gloried on social media, he will then begin to see this as the norm as to how a man should look. And so it is with bathing, staying physically fit, etc. To put it simply, a father or father figure set standards for their children to follow in terms of their physical health and appearance.

In addition, a father should prepare his children physically by encouraging them to be involved in activities that will be beneficial in keeping their bodies fit and healthy. It is important that fathers encourage their children to stay physically active by encouraging them to get involved in sporting activities such as basketball, baseball, football, tennis, etc. Another way a father can instill and prepare his children to stay physically fit is for them to see how important physical fitness is to him personally. This is one thing I can point to with pride that I feel that was imprinted in my children that came from me as their father. I was always into and continue to be into staying physically fit. And I passionately believe this is one of the reasons that my children have a relatively positive attitude toward taking care of themselves physically. It truly warms my heart when I go to my local gym and see a young father with one or more of his kids working out together. He is not only preparing his child toward having a positive attitude toward physical fitness, but it is also a bonding experience for both father and child.

A father must also prepare his children to face life's physical ups and downs. He must teach them that in life, you will always be subject to illnesses that will set you back physically. It's important that a father teaches his children not to give in to short-term physical setbacks that should be a step forward because it prepares and strengthens their child for the next setback. The more a father prepares his children for the physical rigors of life, the better they will be able to face life's ups and downs. There is an acronym that I created that I think emphasizes and summarizes what we all face from the day we are born. The acronym is DAGE which stands for *decay, aging, genetics*, and *environment*. In other words, as long as we live and breathe, we will be subject to constant decay, the aging process that is governed by time, genetic markers we inherit from our parents, and the environment with all of its toxins, bacteria, viruses, and pollution.

In the area of the nutritional preparedness, it is the responsibility of a father to teach his children about proper nutrition. If a child sees their father eating incorrectly, then he shouldn't be surprised when his children adapt a lifestyle of poor nutrition. If bacon and big macs are his best friends, then it should come as no surprise that they will probably be his children's favorite foods as well.

Too many people do not take proper nutrition seriously enough. But the fact of the matter is, if we don't supply our bodies with the proper nutrition on a daily basis, we run the risk of a lifetime of subjecting ourselves to health challenges that could have been avoided if we had just taken control of what we put in our mouths. Again, all fathers should remember that their children are extremely impressionable. If they see daddy having a constant love affair with bacon and all other forms of pork products, then, guess what, pork will be their go-to source of nutrition as well. And even worst, if they see their daddy guzzling down beer or other types of acholic beverages as soon as he comes through the door each evening from work, then it should come as no surprise to him when he finds they are hitting the booze harder than him; they too are on a path of getting their own personal beer guts. And it goes without saying if a child's father is into marijuana (cannabis) or any other illegal substance then, you guessed it, his children may see this type of behavior as something they should embrace too.

Remember, preparing a child requires a deep sense of mentoring with a focus on all of life endeavors. And a real father must be up to the task of steering his children in the right direction even if this sometimes means steering them away from bad habits like eating and drinking the wrong things—things that, in the long run, will be detrimental to their well-being. In other words, a father should not want to be in the habit of passing on his shortcomings to his children but let them (shortcomings) die with him.

In the area of social preparation, it is extremely important that all fathers prepare their children to go forth and face the social issues that they will encounter in their lives. These are social issues which encompass how his children will function as husbands, wives, fathers, mothers, and how they relate to their work associates, family, and friends.

As a real father and a husband, their son(s) must be prepared to take on the responsibility of being the man of their own household. And of course, as wives and mothers, their daughter(s) must be prepared for the responsibilities of becoming the lady of the house in their own future homes.

Social issues preparation includes things like dealing with peer pressure, the proper way to respond to and deal with life's ups downs, and, most importantly, how to deal with the dark forces associated with social media. I say dark forces because in this present day and age, it seems social media is filling our children's minds with a plethora of deviant and harmful ideas on how to live and conduct their lives; it has become a go-to weapon of the enemy of darkness: the devil. To understand how important this issue is, all one must do is look at how fast social media internet sites such as Facebook, Twitter, YouTube, and Instagram have grown in the last ten years. According to infographic,

- Seventy-two percent of all internet users are now active on social media.
- Eighty-nine percent of eighteen to twenty-nine-year-old internet users are active on social media.
- Ninety-three percent of marketers use social media for business.
- Facebook has 1.15 billion monthly active users.

With this ever-increasing use, more and more of our children are now looking to and conducting their lives based on what they see on social media. Social media, in my opinion, is one of the greatest peer pressure that our children face today.

This, of course, all points to the fact that it's a father's responsibility as his children's mentor to teach them the importance of not shaping, conducting, and living their lives based on some random internet advice but from real-life truths that only their father or father figure and his mate can teach them. These are truths that should be scripture-based and grounded in life experiences, not internet opinions and peer pressure.

It's also important to remember that social preparation is closely related to emotional preparation, which will be discussed in detail next, because whatever our social response to different stimuli, so goes our emotions. To discuss our children's social well-being without any regard for how their emotions drive them in terms of their social relationships would be counterproductive. Without your preparation and guidance, your children could possibly live out their lives daily in the social/emotional realms of reacting to and operating from horizontal stimuli such as the social media that indirectly and directly affects their social and emotional well-being.

In addition, given the current media and technology-driven world we now live in, it's important that a father remembers to limit his children's exposure to video games, TV, and cell phone time. Studies have shown on average, children ages two to five spend thirty-two hours a week watching television, cell phones, computers, videos, and using a game console. Children ages six to eleven spend about twenty-eight hours a week in front of the TV, and 97 percent of what they view is live TV. Some of the best ways a father can get his children away from these destructive habits is to schedule quality family time with them such as family game night, family outings, and scheduled date nights (as previously discussed) with just him and them.

A father must emotionally prepare his children by, first and foremost, providing them with a stable and loving home environment. If he and his spouse are constantly at each other's throats in front of his children, then it should come as no surprise that his children will feel emotionally insecure and will manifest that insecurity in a variety of ways. I passionately believe love is a learned behavior. If children see their father as a loving person, particularly to their mother, then they will adapt this behavior and will be loving as well. However, if the opposite is true and they see their father or perceive that he is cold and unemotional, particularly to their mother, then it should come as no surprise that his children will grow up with that same behavior pattern. The display of love and affection is an extremely important emotion for a father to openly embrace. I say this, as I have stated previously, is because most men have an attitude, particularly with their son(s), that to display love and affection is something a strong man just doesn't do; if you hug and kiss your son that you'll, somehow, going to make him weak and effeminate. In other words, real men don't openly display their affection; they keep it in check. Of course, this is just not true. I, for one, wish to this day that my father had shown me some semblance of direct affection. I cannot remember a day in my life when he hugged or said he loved me. He, like most men in his generation, believed that these kinds of emotional displays should be left to women and was part of her motherly duties.

As long as we live and breathe, we all will face the storms of life, so it goes without saying that a father must prepare their children for life's ups and downs. In other words, teach them to be ready for the good and the bad things in life because as long as we all live, we will be either going into a storm, be in a storm, or coming out of a storm; this is a given. However, a father must prepare his children properly on how to deal with life's storms by taking an attitude that this too shall pass, or it just isn't that important, and worry about nothing but instead pray about everything. In addition, a real father understands the importance in teaching his children how to embrace stress relief activities such as exercise, patience, prayer, and putting their faith in the Lord when facing life's ups and downs. If he does, then he has done his job. In Isaiah 40:31 (KJV), we are reminded that "they that wait upon the Lord shall renew their strength; they shall mount up with wings as eagles; they shall run, and not be weary; and they shall walk, and not faint."

All fathers should note that preparing his children intellectually starts while they are still in their mother's womb. He must make sure his children's mother gets the proper prenatal care that is essential for his unborn child's brain cell development; it is just as much his responsibility (as a real father) as it is for their mother.

Studies have also shown that reading, singing, and otherwise communicating with an unborn child can also be beneficial to their intellectual growth. Once a child is born and even before they are born, a real father should be looking at how they are going to fund their future educational pursuits. In addition, a father, along with his mate, must decide whether they want their children to be home, public, or private schooled. Each has its advantages and disadvantages. Preparing his children intellectually also entails him limiting his children's access to unproductive activities, as previously discussed, such as too much TV watching, video game playing, etc.; instead, they need to get their children in the habit of reading more, participating in mind-building hobbies, and more studying. Remember, there is no such thing as an unmotivated child; you just have to find what interest them and allow them an opportunity to explore and expand their interest in whatever most motivates them.

Finally, all fathers must prepare their children on how to manage their finances. It is the duty of every parent and, particularly the father figure in their lives, to empower their children with financial wisdom. This starts with their father, their number one role model, showing them by way of example as to what wise financial stewardship looks like. If a child sees their parents making wise decisions about money, then they will grow up with an eye for wise financial stewardship as well. He must teach them how important it is to not only earn a good living but how to properly allocate what they earn. A real father starts by teaching his children the importance of a budget, which is defined as simply balancing your expenses with your income. Or to put it another way, it is telling your money what to do in advance instead of wondering what happened to your money after it's gone. Since budgeting starts with income, it's a good idea that a father starts his children off at an early age with the ability to earn their own income. In most cases, parents simply give their children an allowance which doesn't really work well as a learning tool because you run the risk of a child growing up with an entitlement attitude. A better way to prepare them on how to handle their finances is by giving them a chance to practice what you preach. A father can do this by letting them earn and manage their own money. For example, rather than giving them an allowance, let them work for a commission. Set up a list of household chores and then pay them a commission at the completion of the chore. By letting a child earn money versus giving them an allowance teaches them to appreciate the fruits of their labor rather than just feeling entitled. In addition, it is never too early to teach a child about and how to invest for the future. They need to understand that investing for the future, in its simplest terms, involves saving enough discretionary funds and then investing them in a long-term mutual fund, growth stocks, or real estate that have high yield potentials of return over time. For example, if you had invested five thousand in amazon stocks in 1997, that five-thousand-dollar investment would have grown to four million dollars in 2017!

In addition, it is extremely important, and something I can't stress enough, that all real fathers must demonstrate first by example and then by instruction the importance of staying out of debt. Remember you can't save and invest if you're always in debt. Scripture reminds us "the borrower is servant to the lender," and if you want your children to be good stewards over that which God entrust them with and have a life full of financial freedom, it must be one free from debt and knowledge on how to budget, save, and invest wisely.

To sum it all up, all real fathers must prepare their children for what comes next, and it all starts at the time their children are born; they, as the pilot of their family along with their copilot, must pick a safe and nurturing neighborhood that has good schools with career-centered goals and with an opportunity for their children to grow up with peers who value education, hard work, and achievement. If you don't think this advice is important, let me share with you again the challenges I had to overcome based on the environment I was raised in. To start, I was born into a poverty-stricken family, the tenth child in a family of twelve children. In my early years, I was raised in a poor public-project neighborhood in the northeast section of Washington, DC. As I have stated before, my father could best be described as an absentee father because by the time I came along, he was no longer living with my mother and my siblings. Each day was simply an exercise in survival. Food, clothing, and adequate shelter were not easy to come by.

The neighborhood school that I attended as a child was a public school geared toward project kids. It employed teachers with no sympathy or empathy for the kids they were charged to teach. Kids that were suffering from a lack of basic needs such as food, clothing, and proper shelter. As I look back, I now realize these lack of the basic needs as well as an absentee father all contributed to the fact that I was placed in school at the age of seven thus setting me back one school year in my formative education. And then based primarily on continued extreme poverty, I subsequently had to repeat the third grade. This, all of which, contributed to the fact that I did not graduate from high school until I was nearly twenty years of age.

It bears repeating that when a man takes on the responsibility of fatherhood and if he genuinely wants to become a real father, he must be ready and able to prepare his children for the challenges of life that will involve their spiritual, physical, nutritional, social, emotional, intellectual, and financial well-being.

Fatherhood Quiz

1. What are the five preparing areas of endeavors that a father should teach his children?
   a.
   b.
   c.
   d.
   e.

2. What does the acronym DAGE represent?

3. According to infographic, what percent of internet users are now active on social media?

4. Why is it important for a father to express and show love not only to his daughter(s) but also to his son(s)?

CHAPTER 6

Pillar 5—The Praising Father

Praise is like sunlight to the human spirit: we cannot flower and grow without it.

—Jess Lair

When I think of praise and what a powerful influence it has on people, especially the young mind, I immediately think of my high school football playing days and my high school football coach. I was finishing up my last year of high school and played the wide receiver and defensive end position on our football team. Our team was facing our final game of the season; all we had to do to make it to the city championship game was to defeat a team that had never defeated my school's football team in the entire history of our school, and they were yet again in another losing streak. Needless to say, we were heavily favored to win the game and, as a team, feeling a little overconfident or, should I say in retrospect, really overconfident! Because of this overconfidence, we didn't put our best foot forward and found ourselves losing at half time. So what did our coach say to the team during his half-time locker-room speech (which should have been a pep talk)? He said, "You're going to lose," and then he turned around and walked out of the locker room. Needless to say, our spirits now crushed, his words or lack of praise and support became a self-fulfilling prophecy, and you guessed it: we lost.

In the next three chapters, starting with this chapter, I will be discussing the maintenance pillars. The praise, patience, and prayer pillars make up these last three pillars and represent the pillars that all fathers must learn to utilize throughout their children's lives particularly after they leave the nest.

When you ask most folks what motivates them, they will tell you it's money. But research has shown that praise and recognition are really the greatest motivators. If you don't believe this is true, just think of all of the rich people who have more money than they could ever hope for, yet they still crave recognition and praise. Two good examples of people who have more than enough money but continue to obsess over more and more praise and recognition is President Donald J. Trump, the forty-fifth president of the United States, and Kanye West. In the case of Donald Trump, even while he held the highest office in the land, he continued to try to boost his ego by professing his own greatness on Twitter and in the press on a daily basis. And in the case of Kanye West, on the surface, it appears he has everything any man could ever hope for: more money than he could ever spend, a beautiful wife, fame, and four beautiful children. Yet he continues to seek praise and recognition by constantly recreating himself. Being a recording artist was not enough to keep his ego satisfied because, just recently, he decided, in an effort to get even more recognition, he would take on a religious persona and hold his own Sunday services with him being the center of attraction. His need for praise and recognition has also led him to even announce and run for president of the United States. Although the examples given are men with overinflated runaway egos, it still points to one important factor: just as grown men with wealth and fame continue to seek praise and recognition to boost their self-esteem, it is also a fundamental need that all children have—a need that comes, first and foremost, from their father. That need being praise and recognition that helps to boost and build their self-esteem.

A real father knows how to instill self-esteem in his children through encouragement, support, and positive affirmations. A real father also recognizes that a healthy self-esteem helps his children feel secure and worthwhile. It helps them to build positive relationships with others and feel confident about their abilities. It also helps them to be open to learning and feedback, which can help them acquire and master new skills.

Research has also shown that praising and encouraging children helps them accomplish general everyday tasks during early childhood years especially when they are achieving new goals such as learning to walk, eating vegetables, or sitting still for physical exams. This points to the fact that to motivate your child, you don't need to reward them each time they do something well.

Children can become self-motivated when their natural curiosity is encouraged and supported, and they tend to do things simply because they enjoy doing them. Children who are self-motivated have better mental health and well-being than those who rely on being rewarded by others to feel good about themselves.

Fathers need to be aware that they can negatively influence their children's motivation by making them feel they need a reward every time they do something right; as a consequence, they may avoid activities, and this can lead to a reduce sense of control and lowered self-esteem.

Gaining approval from important adults, such as their father or father figure, in their lives becomes more important to children as they grow. Praise is more effective when it is specific and when parents and love ones are mindful of how and when they praise. Praise that is specific and acknowledges the processes of completing an activity or solving a problem helps develop children's learning and motivation. Examples of specific praise are, "You put away your toys nicely," or "Well done in eating all your dinner," or "Thank you for coming home when you agreed that you would."

Praise should be given mindfully and in consideration of a child's age and stage of development as well as their individual ability.

Children cannot imprint from their parents when they are not genuine, especially if the parent used the same words of praise repeatedly. The timing of praise is also important; interrupting a child when they are concentrating can make them lose their focus and reduce their motivation to continue with the given activity.

Praise is also effective in encouraging children, especially older children, to relate to how they feel about who they are and to their achievements; praise also encourages positive self-esteem and self-worth.

Further research also indicates that instilling and building a child's self-esteem is important to all ages but is even more essential during a child's formative years. This research emphasized the following seven helpful tips to utilize when it comes to building a child's self-esteem:

1. *When you feel good about your child, say so.* Try to give them words of encouragement each day. The little things you say can add up over time and have a major effect on your children.
2. *Always be on the lookout for small changes and accomplishments.* Do not wait until your child has done something good to give a compliment; every effort or improvement should be praised.
3. *Try not to practice a leave alone zap attitude toward your children.* In other words, praise them more than you criticize them. Do not ignore things that they do good and only say something to them when they do something wrong. As a guide, praise them six times more than you criticize them; make sure even when you criticize them that you always leave them with some type of positive affirmation. For example, suppose your child gets into trouble in school, you should, of course, chastise your child for their wrongdoing but immediately follow up by letting them know that they are better than the bad behavior they are displaying and encourage them to do better.
4. *Recognize that not everyone is the same, and you should praise your child for their unique strengths and encourage them to develop and feel excited about their interest.* This means that just because an activity does not interest you, there is no reason to ignore it just because it is something that interest your child and not you. For example, you're into sporting activities like football and baseball, but your son is interested in drone racing or robot building; it's important

to show interest in whatever activities your children like because this will help them develop a sense of pride and confidence.
5. *Surprise your child with a reward for good behavior.* For example, say something like, "Thanks for picking up the toys; let's go to the park to celebrate." This, of course, is utilizing the principles of operant conditioning or positive reinforcement. By rewarding positive behavior encourages the repeating of the desired behavior.
6. *Praise effort as well as achievement.* Recognize how hard your child is trying—for example, "You really worked hard on that essay," or "Thank you for remembering to hang up your coat. It's always important to recognize the amount of work, time, and effort your child puts into all their endeavors.
7. *Try to make your praise dependent on your child's behavior rather than your feelings.* This may seem hard, at times, because you may feel that some of the positive behavior they display in your eyes is no big deal. However, in their eyes, it may be a huge deal.

In terms of the female child, encouragement, support, and positive affirmation takes on a different dynamic in comparison to her male counterpart. In the case of the female child, she has an innate need to be affirmed by a male, particularly during her formative years; if she doesn't get that affirmation from her father (or father figure), her self-esteem may suffer. She will seek out and run the risk of being abused by a predator male that is full of hidden agendas unlike her father who possesses unconditional love for her. Remember, a daughter needs her father—prayerfully a real father, a loving father—to be the standard against which she can use to judge all men.

In the case of the male child, his father is, first and foremost, seen as his number one hero unless of course he has an absentee father or an overly abusive father. Then he becomes an enemy rather than a hero in their eyes. The greatest praise a son can get is from his earthly father. I cannot stress this point enough: to operate as a real father, a man should never underestimate the importance of being involved in the major events of his children's lives. In far too many cases, without the praise and support from their fathers, many male children turn to the streets for what might be missing from their home environment with disastrous results. This author can testify to these things based on his own personal experience with the loss of his only son to the streets of Washington, DC. The loss of my son at the hands of a gunman and knowing I possibly could have steered him in a different direction if only I had praised, supported, and spent more quality time with him, especially during his formative years, will haunt me for the rest of my life. A father should never ever put a job or anything else over the emotional needs and love of his children.

What is equally as important as praising and supporting your children is to refrain from overly criticizing them. Far too many men think that it is their duties to verbally and, sometimes, even physically abuse their children, particularly their male children, in an effort to discipline them. The effects of overly criticizing a child during their formative years can be something that can be extremely detrimental to them and life changing. It can negatively impact their self-esteem for the rest of their lives.

This over criticizing, I think, was beautifully illustrated in the motion picture movie titled *Fences* starring Denzel Washington. In the movie, Denzel plays the role of a father that has difficulty in finding or saying anything good about his young teenage son. He berates and threatens his son when he approaches him with his dreams of pursuing a college education that could be financed by a football scholarship. Part of the reason why Denzel (the father) did not support his son's dream was because of his own past failure as an athlete and not getting a chance to fulfill his dreams; it was coupled with the fact that this was the way his father treated him. This points to an important and old detrimental fathering habit that if not put to rest by all fathers and father figures will simply be passed on to future generations. I can testify from my own personal experience how detrimental over criticizing a child can affect a child. Real fathering requires a tremendous amount of praising coupled with patience.

As I stated previously, after the passing of my mother, when I was only nine years old, I was first passed from one older sister and then to another. As I approached my preteen years, I found myself in the care of one of my older sisters who already had her hands full with eight kids of her own. To add insult to injury, she was married to not only a verbally and physically abusive man but also a man that was an atheist. My brother-in-law would attack my self-esteem on a regular basis with disparaging remarks such as, "You're weak, and you're never be a real man." He constantly pitted me against my other brothers. And to make matters worse, this was my first father figure because at this time in my life, as I have stated previously, my biological father was an absentee father that lived with his second wife on the other side of the city. This type of over criticizing is, of course, not just limited to male children; it also occurs, far too often, with female children as well.

My wife's father was also an abusive, over-criticizing father. He would, on a regular basis particularly if he had a bad day at work, come home with a bad attitude and displaced his anger on his children and their mother. His abusive behavior affected her and her three siblings in different ways but was most harmful to her oldest sister and only brother whose self-esteems still suffers to this day. As my wife explained it to me, her older sister's self-esteem problems started when she was a young child; she would overhear her father discussing with her mother how he felt she was weak, and people will take advantage of weak girls. These and many other incidents, even though she's now in her fifties, has caused her to continue to doubt her self-worth. This self-esteem problem, in my opinion, is one of the underlying reasons that has hindered her ability to successfully relate to any man for any length of time. Her brother, because of the emotional and sometimes physical abuse he suffered from his father, has doubted his self-worth and has a hard time expressing his inner feelings.

To better understand how important a father's praise and support is to child's self-esteem and well-being, all one has to do is to take a look at what the social scientist refers to as the Pygmalion or Rosenthal effect; it explains the phenomenon whereby other's expectations of a target person affect the targets person's performance. And the opposite known as the Golem effect leads to decrease in performance; both effects are forms of self-fulfilling prophecy. To put it another way, these effects point to the fact that a man's children will tend to perform up to the level of performance he expects of them. Once a child's father or father figure set expectations for his children, good or bad, that is what their children will tend to live up to which, in turn, becomes self-fulfilling prophecies.

In addition, confidence is closely related to praising and support because confidence is the result of praising and supporting. Confidence is defined as the feeling or belief that one can rely on someone or something—a feeling of self-assurance arising from one's appreciation of one's own abilities or qualities. By praising and supporting his children, a father helps them to build confidence in themselves that helps them to believe in themselves and feel comfortable in their true self knowing they have worth. If his children develop confidence in themselves, people will sense this confidence. Confidence is attractive and invites success because it helps people to connect to others. Remember praise = support = encouragement = confidence =pride in self. In other words, when a father praises his children, he is supporting and showing confidence in their dreams which encourages a sense of pride in self. And with a healthy self-esteem and self-image, his children can face and conquer anything that life may place in their paths.

Finally, a word of caution in terms of too much praise. Studies have shown that too much praise of any sort can be unhealthy. Research has found that students who were lavished with praise were more cautious in their responses to questions, had less confidence in their answers, less persistent in difficult assignments, and less willing to share their ideas. The studies also found that too much praise to a child is like a bad habit that is hard to break. Once they get it, they need it, and they want more. Unfortunately, the real world does not praise them for just doing a basic thing like getting dressed in the morning. New research goes on to say that too much praise for children as young as one to three can have negative repercussions in the future.

A study done by Columbia University researchers Claudia Miller & Carol Dweck found that children who were praised for their intelligence as compared to their effort became overly focused on results. Based on these findings, the researchers suggest you should avoid praising your children about areas over which they have no control. This includes any innate and unalterable ability such as intelligence, physical attractiveness, athletic or artistic gifts. You should direct your praise to areas over which your children have control—things like effort, attitude, responsibility, commitment, discipline, focus, decision-making, compassion, generosity, respect, and love. Further, according to Dr. Jim Taylor, PhD, "Praising children for intelligence makes them fear difficulty because they begin to equate failure with stupidity."

The bottom line is this: children do not need to be told "good job" or any of the other pet clichés when they have done something well; it is self-evident. They do, however, need to be told why they did well so they can replicate that behavior in the future to get the same positive outcome. This, of course, is the essence of operant conditioning. Operant conditioning is defined as "a type of associative learning process through which the strength of a behavior is modified by reinforcement or punishment." Remember, if a father wants to get the best behavior from his children, he must, as a real father, recognize the power of praise and support. Praise and support are some of the most simple and useful reinforcement tools that every real father should have in their fatherly toolbox.

THE SEVEN PILLARS OF FATHERHOOD

Fatherhood Quiz

1. What are five helpful tips (seven were given) a father can utilize when it comes to building his children's self-esteem?
   a.
   b.
   c.
   d.
   e.

CHAPTER 7

Pillar 6—The Patient Father

Parents don't come down too hard on your children or you'll crush their spirits.
—Colossians 3:21 (NIV)

Have you ever found yourself rushing into something that you later regretted? Then welcome to the family! I think we all have been in this position at one time or another. We rushed in, for example, the buying of a new car by some slick salesman and then realized if you had been patient and did your due diligence, you could have gotten a better deal and saved thousands of dollars. In fact, just recently, I purchased a new vehicle, and after months of research, price comparing, and patience, I was able to save $11,000 off the sticker price. To broker a deal like this, I had to patiently wait out the dealer for over a month after presenting them with what I felt was a fair price and what I was willing to pay. Of course, it was not what they wanted me to pay. Another example of impatience costing a person to spend too much and occurs far too often is when they rush into buying a house they cannot afford and then wound up losing the house through foreclosure.

In the neighborhood that I have currently lived in for over the last twenty years, I have seen this scenario played out repeatedly. Folks buy a house knowing they cannot really afford to pay the mortgage, and then they try to salvage the situation by refinancing the house over and over only to finally face foreclosure. We all know of folks that have rushed impatiently into a marriage for all the wrong reasons only to find themselves in divorce court within a matter of a few years or even months after saying I do. These are only a few examples of impatience which, in far too many cases, stem from parents that did not teach their children the value of patience which relates to discipline which relates to self-control which relates to misbehaving. You see, when a parent, and particularly a father, fails to teach their children how to be patient, their children, in far too many cases, will lack the discipline to practice self-control and find themselves making bad impulsive decisions. Impatience, at its core, can lead to a life that is driven by the mantra, "I got to get mine now, not later." This causes far too many young people to get involved in illegal activities such as drug dealing, robbery, and other illegal activities. They have never been taught that "hastened speculation leads to poverty; Scripture reminds us in Galatians 6:7 (KJV), "Be not deceived; God is not mocked: for whatsoever a man soweth, that shall he also reap." And it's every real father's responsibility, as their children's mentor, to teach them the concept and value of patience. Given the fact that *patience* is one of the three maintenance pillars makes it a concept that must be emphasized not just during his children's formative years but every day of their lives as they face daily decisions in an impatient, urgency-addicted, money-driven, capitalistic society. Remember, "to lose patience is to lose the battle" (Mahatma Gandhi).

We have all heard the old quote patience is a virtue and recognize the importance of being patient in certain situations, as stated previously; however, patience when it comes to raising children can be seen as so much more than just a virtue.

Patience can be defined as "the capacity to accept or tolerate trouble or suffering without getting angry or upset." When you examine this definition, one can easily see that patience requires the ability to withstand difficult situations without losing control. Or to put it another way, a large part of patience is power under control, which of course is the definition for meekness. Patience is also an important tool in overcoming frustration. Patience allows us to suspend judgement long enough to make informed decisions which helps to pave the way to a peaceful and joyous life. According to Vandana Singhal, there are five reasons why patience should be emphasized and practiced:

1. *Patience shapes a talent into achievement.* To shape your talents and inborn abilities into real achievements, you must have patience.
2. *Patience transforms relationships.* If we do not recognize the importance of patience, we make hasty decisions. Whenever you feel defensive against a person, try to be patient enough to take time to think over another person's positive qualities.
3. *Patience helps you to be empathetic.* Building empathy toward others is especially important if you want to live a hassle-free life.
4. *Patience helps acquire positive attitude.* To avoid frustration, you must learn to be patient and see things and situations in a positive light to make your life happier. And to get that positivity, you need to be patient.
5. *Patience makes you healthier.* Anger and stress are two things that are enough to ruin a person's health. And patience is the antidote to both these illnesses.

In addition, recent studies have found that good things really do come to those who wait. Science-backed benefits include the following:

1. Patient people enjoy better mental health.
2. Patience helps us achieve our goals.
3. Patient people are better friends and neighbors.
4. Patience is linked to good health.

Again, patience is so much more than a virtue especially in terms of raising children. Children require not only patience but understanding. If a father loses his cool in a given situation, it could possibly mean he will lose the love and respect of his child. It's more prudent and wiser to go to prayer and assess any given situation from a calm spiritually derived perspective.

A godly real father is meek and slow to anger. He knows the difference between alienating his children and how to firmly direct his children in the right direction. Scriptures reminds us that "in your anger do not sin; do not let the sun go down while you are still angry, and do not give the devil a foothold" (Ephesian 4:26–27 NIV). In addition, it bears repeating, anger and stress are enough to ruin a person's health; patience is the cure for both.

Being patient may come easy to some, but in far too many cases, particularly when it comes to raising children as stated previously, too many fathers lose their tempers and wound up causing their children to resent and even hate them as a father. The media is full of stories of fathers that have lost control of their tempers and abused their children. Remember, when the man of the house loses control, the whole house is out of control. That's why it is so vitally important that even in the most heated situations, all fathers must learn to step back, cool down, and consult with their Creator; if they don't, their anger can and will get the best of them with life-changing consequences. Ephesian 6:4 (NLT) reminds us, "Fathers, do not provoke your children to anger by the way you treat them. Rather bring them up with discipline and instruction that comes from the Lord."

Remember these life-changing consequences include alienating children to the point that they may resent and even hate their father; an even more frightening consequence is the fact that this unrestrained anger can cause children to take a path in life that could include criminal activities and even abuse of their own children. Scripture reminds us, "My dear brothers and sisters, take note of this: everyone should be quick to listen, slow to speak and slow to become angry for a man's anger does not bring the righteous life that God deserves" (James 1:19–20 NIV).

Patience is also closely related to discipline. And discipline is defined as "the practice of training people to obey rules or a code of behavior using punishment to correct disobedience." A godly real father knows that in order to direct his children away from disobedience, he must learn to use punishment at the correct time and situation. For example, it is far better to use corporate punishment on a young child immediately after the infraction. It serves no purpose to tell a two-year-old that you are going to spank them as soon as you get back to the house because they acted up in the store while you were out shopping. Because at this age, they will simply think you are punishing them for no real reason because in their young minds, they have completely forgotten what they did earlier at the store.

I remember when my youngest daughter was three years old, and she did something bad, and I chastised her, and then not too long after the infraction, she came to me and wanted me to play with her even though I was still a little upset with her. And because I was reluctant to play with her, she became upset with me because, at the age of three, she did not understand why I was still upset with her. In fact, she went to my wife and asked her why I was still upset with her. And even though my wife explained to her why I was still upset with her, she was still perplexed. In fact, later, while I was working in my office, she decided to write me a sweet little letter that only a three-year-old could write (a letter which I still have to this day); it asked me why I was still mad at her and that she was sorry even though I knew deep down she did not know what she was sorry for. Nonetheless, because she thought I was still upset, she decided to apologize by way of a little letter in hopes that it would get my attention, and it did, of course. But in her mind, the issue that made her daddy upset with her in the first place was over before it even started. You see, in her young mind, once she said she was sorry, there was no reason for any further bad feelings on my part. The lesson to be learned here is that babies do not dwell on the past like adults. This is probably something we all should learn from them, and remember that the past is the past, and it is better to forgive and forget. In addition, as noted, when a child does do something wrong no matter how bad it may be, they see the infraction totally different than we do as an adult.

As your children mature and approach preteen and beyond, corporate punishment becomes, for all practical purposes, useless. For example, I can remember a story that was shared with my wife by one of our church members when she tried to discipline her thirteen-year-old son after he got in trouble for something he did at school. Keep in mind her thirteen-year-old son was almost six feet tall, and she only stands approximately five feet tall. She ordered him to lie across his bed in an attempt to spank him, and he announced to her after she tried spanking him, "Ma, you know that doesn't hurt," and after exhausting herself trying to discipline him by way of corporate punishment, she quickly realized her efforts were in vain. A much better punishment at this age would have been to take something away from her son that was important to him. For example, if he loved to play video games, then taking away this privilege would have served as a better punishment for his bad behavior instead of spanking.

The bottom line is this: no matter what the age of your child, when dealing with their discipline, you must keep in mind their discipline is causally related to how you practice and embrace patience. If a father loses his patience with his children, particularly after they do something stupid, as a parent, he must learn to practice patience because if he loses control, he runs the risk of losing his children's chance to learn what true discipline looks like. True discipline is always coupled with unconditional love and patience.

An excellent example of a father's patience coupled with love can be seen in the biblical story of the prodigal son or the lost. It's summarized as follows: There was once a man who had two sons. The younger son said to his father, "Father, I want right now what's coming to me. So the father divided the property between them. It was not long before the younger son packed his bags and left for a distant country. There, undisciplined and dissipated, he wasted everything he had. After he had gone through all his money, there was a bad famine all throughout that country, and he began to hurt. He signed on with a citizen there who assigned him to his fields to slop the pigs. He was so hungry he would have eaten the corncobs in the pig slop, but no one would give him any. That bought him to his senses. He spoke, "All those farmhands working for my father sit down to three meals a day, and here I am starving to death. I am going back to my father. I will say to him, 'Father, I have sinned against God. I have sinned before you. I do not deserve to be called your son. Take me on as a hired hand.'" He got right up and went home to his father. When he was still a long way off, his father saw him. His heart pounding, he ran out, embraced him, and kissed him. The son started his speech: "Father, I've sinned against God. I've sinned before you. I don't deserve to be called your son ever again." But the father was not listening. He was calling to his servants, "Quick, bring a clean set of clothes and dress him. Put the family ring on his finger and sandals on his feet. Then get a grain-fed heifer and roast it. We are going to feast! We are going to have a wonderful time! My son is here given up for dead and now alive! Given up for lost and now found!" And they began to have a wonderful time. This father rejoiced because his son who was dead because of sin was now alive and no longer given up as lost to sin. I am sure this father rejoiced also in the fact that his prayers were answered by the loving God of all creation.

This biblical parable is an excellent example of a father who practiced patience, unconditional love, and, upon his son's return, praise and support for an undisciplined child. He was patient enough to wait for his son to mature and come to his senses and realize that his undisciplined impatient attitude had led him down a path of destruction. He also never lost hope that his son would return to him one day, and his unconditional love for his son sustained this hope. So it is with our heavenly Father who, because of his unconditional love for his earthly children, never gives up on them no matter how sinful and out of control they may become. Because He knows as with the prodigal son and Paul—who was an archenemy of all Christians until he came to the knowledge of the truth in Jesus Christ as he traveled on the road to Damascus—that even the greatest of sinners can be redeemed as long as they have breath in their bodies.

Ultimately, one of the best examples of a patient father at his greatest at work even though his children are continually misbehaving (as demonstrated in the parable of the lost son) is our heavenly Father who justly deserves to be called "Abba, Father" which is Aramaic for "Daddy." Scripture reminds us when you state Abba, Father, you are envisioning a father or daddy who knows your greatest strengths and your greatest weaknesses—a father or daddy who knows your beginning and end; instead of forcing His will on you,

He allows you to meet Him in your own way—with intimacy that can only be felt between the Creator and the created. If our heavenly Father is patient and loving enough to continually put up with all of his creations' (you and I) disobedience and shortcomings, then we should learn from his example and learn and practice patience with our earthly children.

A godly directed real father must continually strive to understand his children's greatest strengths and weaknesses—a father who, because of his wisdom, can see his children's possible beginnings and ends but is still wise enough and patient enough to not force his will on his children. He recognizes how important it is to allow his children to meet him in their own way with the love and intimacy that can only come from their father. And he understands how to cultivate patience by reframing situations, practicing mindfulness, and gratitude.

Finally, if you don't take away anything else from this chapter, remember patience is so much more than virtue; it is a discipline that, if not embraced, can mean the difference between a father boosting his children's spirit or crushing it and, in the process, losing their friendship, love, and respect. Children must be raised with patience, understanding, and kindness in a loving and nurturing home environment. Remember, "One moment of patience may ward off a great disaster. One moment of impatience may ruin a whole life" (Chinese Proverb).

DONALD H. WOOD, PH.D

Fatherhood Quiz

1. Why is patience so much more than a virtue, especially in terms of raising children?

2. What lessons can we learn from the story of the prodigal son in terms of raising children?

3. How would you define patience?

4. Why is it so important to teach your children patience?

5. What are some of the dangers of not teaching your children patience?

CHAPTER 8

Pillar 7—The Praying Father

Then you will call on me and come pray to me, and I will listen to you.
—Jeremiah 29:12 (NIV)

Ask yourself this question, What would you do if your eighteen-year-old daughter comes to you and tells you that she has decided to drop out of college and marry her incarcerated boyfriend, or if one of your children have decided, for whatever reason, they are atheist? In situations like these, not only patience but also prayer may be your only go-to response that you, as a loving father, are left with.

A godly real father knows how to be a prayer warrior on behalf of his children and ready to lift his children up in prayer in all that they do while praying for godly direction and protection. If we take a look at Scripture, not only did God state, "Then you will call on me and come pray to me, and I will listen to you" (Jeremiah 29:12 NIV). We also see that in Scripture, Job understood the importance of praying for his children and made prayer and sacrifice on their behalf a regular practice. To summarize, Job found his sons used to take turns holding feast in their homes, and they would invite their three sisters to eat and drink with them. When a period of feasting (partying) had run its course, Job would send and have them purified. Early in the morning he would sacrifice burnt offerings for each of them thinking, *Perhaps my children have sinned and cursed God in their hearts.* This was Job's regular custom (Job 1:4–5 NIV). Unfortunately, in far too many cases, with some children who have become completely immersed in the sins of this world, prayer becomes a godly father's only go-to weapon to protect them and not only to protect them from sin but also to keep them out of harm's way.

How many real fathers, like myself, have sat up at night wondering and worrying when our teenage son or daughter was coming home after a night of partying or just hanging out with their friends. We find no peace until we know that our children are safely back in the house. In fact, I can remember when my youngest daughter first started driving at the age of sixteen and how I would continually check on her and, yes, worry about her when she was out and about by herself. As with most loving and concerned fathers raising a teenager, I would give her a specific time to be back in the house, reasoning that nothing good happens to a young girl as the night hours progressed, but, of course, she would not adhere to my time constraints causing me to worry even more. My wife would even laugh at me at times because she would tell me, "You're going to let that girl worry you to death. You can stay up, but I'm going to bed." But no matter what she said, I would not go to sleep until she was safety back in the house. Situations like this reminded me that becoming a father means you are in store for lifetime of worry. It just comes with the territory, so to speak. However, there's a correct and incorrect way to respond to these situations, and knowing the difference can make life so much easier.

It also important to note that even after your children are grown and leave your protection to live on their own, all real fathers still worry. For example, when they tell you they are going to visit another country for vacation purposes or they join the military, and you know they may be placed in harm's way. The first thing that comes to mind for many fathers including me is the movie titled *Taken*, starring Liam Neeson, who portrays a father whose teenage daughter goes on a European vacation with her best friend, and they are subsequently abducted by slave trade predators. Neeson goes into action and goes to extreme measures to find and save his daughter. In fact, he could not rest until he made sure his daughter was safe and no longer in harm's way. It is only natural for a loving real father to worry about his children no matter how old they get. In the same way, our heavenly Father is concerned with our well-being until we come home to be with him. Although it is a well-used quote and scripturally-based and is easier said than done, particularly as a loving and caring father, one should always remember, "Do not be anxious about anything, but in every situation, by prayer and petition, with thanksgiving, present your requests to God" (Philippians 4:6 NIV).

Prayer is the third and final maintenance pillar. It is the final pillar that a father must embrace and utilize throughout his children's lives no matter what their age. A real father knows that no matter how old his children get, they are and always will be his babies.

The first question that must be addressed in terms of prayer is, Why do we need to pray? Too many people, and particularly men, think the purpose of prayer is to ask God for stuff or to help us when our lives take a turn for the worst. But the real purpose of prayer is for us to conform or submit to God's will. This is why it's important to always end all prayers by stating—as found in the model prayer, the Lord's Prayer—"not your will be done but his will be done." We are not to pray to change God but for prayer to change us. When we pray, we are seeking a deeper personal relationship with our Creator. If we don't continue to develop a deeper relationship with God, we will get caught up in the ways of the world and lose our faith in our Creator. Living a life apart from our creator ultimately leads to a life that is empty of true peace and joy.

It has been my experience that many men not only don't see the need or value in prayer but also don't even know how to pray. If you think this is not so, just think about what happens at the dinner table at thanksgiving or other holidays events when most families start their meals off with prayer. In most cases, family members, especially the men, look to a man in the family whom they assume is a follower of Christ to lead the family in prayer; they secretly hope they will never be called on to do the same because the concept of prayer is foreign to them and feel they simply don't know or have never been taught how to pray. In fact, the survey I conducted in research for the writing of this book revealed that most of the survey respondents (especially the men) when asked the question, Were you raised by a praying, God-fearing, and spirit-filled father? They responded no.

Now let's take a closer look at what exactly is prayer. Well to start, prayer can be defined as "a solemn request for help or an expression of thanks addressed to God or an object of worship" or simply talking or communicating with God. Although prayer is simply talking to our Creator, there are some fundamental guidelines that can be utilized to make your prayers more effectual. It's important to remember that the Lord only responds to the effectual prayers of the righteous. Scripture reminds us, "The effectual fervent prayer of a righteous man availeth much" (James 5:16 KJV). Now let us take a closer look at this scripture by first defining what is effectual prayer. According to *The Merriam-Webster Dictionary*, effectual is defined as "producing or able to produce a desired effect." From a biblical standpoint, according to World Vision speaker Marilee Pierce Dunker based on Luke 5:16 (AMP), effectual prayer involves eight key components:

1. *Know to whom you are speaking.* Because prayer is simply having a conversation with our Creator, your prayer should begin with addressing the person to whom you are speaking by name.
2. *Thank him.* It is always a good idea to start your prayers with a heartfelt thank you to your Lord and Savior and benefactor. Praise opens the gates of heaven and should always be part of our alone time with God.
3. *Ask for God's will.* Prayer should never be about our will being done but God's will being done because our heavenly Father always knows what is best for us even though we may think we know better.
4. *Say what you need.* Whether the need is large or small, the Lord is always willing to listen to all our request and delights to give you good gifts. The Bible says, "You do not have because you do not ask God."
5. *Ask for forgiveness.* A repentant heart is necessary if we want our prayers to be heard by the Lord. James 5:16 reminds us

that if we want our prayers to be heard, our hearts need to be right with God and with one another.
6. *Pray with a friend.* There is power in praying with a trusted friend.
7. *Pray the Word.* The Word of God has power and a great spiritual weapon.
8. *Memorize Scripture.* The only way to understand our spiritual authority in Christ is to become intimately familiar with the Scriptures. Just a few minutes a day will add strength and authority to your prayer life.

Now let us take a closer look at the word *fervent*. According to *Merriam-Webster Dictionary*, the word *fervent* is defined as "exhibiting or marked by great intensity of feeling." And the biblical definition defines fervent as "having or showing great warmth or intensity of spirit, feeling, enthusiasm, etc." So from these definitions, we can see that when we pray, we should pray with great warmth, intensity of spirit, feeling, and enthusiasm.

Finally, let us take a closer look at the word *righteous* in terms of our prayer requests. According to the dictionary, righteous simply means "to be right, especially in a moral way." From a scriptural perspective, a righteous person is in right standing or in right relationship with God.

All prayers should contain the following basic elements: adoration, confession, thanksgiving, and supplication. The model prayer (the Lord's Prayer) that Jesus taught his disciples included all of these elements. The prayer included the following passages, "Our father which art in heaven hallow would be thy name. Thy kingdom come, thy will be done, on earth as it is in heaven. Give us this day our daily bread and thine is the kingdom the power and the glory." All of which demonstrates adoration for the Lord of lords. "Forgive us our trust passes as we forgive those who have trust passed against us" demonstrates confession, and the passages "give us this day our daily bread and lead us not into temptation but deliver us from evil" demonstrates thanksgiving and supplication.

Another way to look at and remember the basic components of prayer is in terms of an acronym postulated by Dr. R. C. Sproul. In the acronym we find the following: The *A* in ACTS represents adoration, which means when we pray to God, we must always acknowledge that He is the God of all creation and worthy of all honor and glory. The *C* in ACTS represents confession, which means when we pray to God, we must always confess and repent of all our sins and transgressions to a holy and righteous God. The *T* in ACTS represents thanksgiving, which means when we pray to God, we must always thank God for the endless blessings He honors us with each day. And finally, the *S* in ACTS represents supplication, which means this is the part of the prayer where you can humbly ask the Lord for help and intercession.

Remember, prayer is a powerful weapon that not only fathers should embrace but also something all parents should learn to embrace. And praying is not just something that only women or religious people do; it is something that every real father should do daily on the behalf of their family and children. Never underestimate the power of prayer because God's presence has the power to make dramatic differences in a father and his children's lives. The Lord is always ready to hear all our concerns no matter how large or small they may be. In addition, prayer does not have to be lengthy. The Lord's Prayer consist of exactly sixty-six words in the King James version. In contrast, the Declaration of Independence is comprised of 1,322 words. All of which tells us the power of prayer does not depend on the length of the prayer but rather how heartfelt and sanctified the prayer is.

A good example of a man who understands and appreciates the power of prayer is my pastor, Pastor Michael R. White. I say this because I recall one Saturday morning while he was teaching a men's fellowship and his son was in attendance but had to leave early to return to his college campus, my Pastor—being a real father in every sense of the word—before his son left to make the trip back to campus, immediately stopped what he was doing and said, "We need to pray for my son's safe travel back to his college." Pastor White recognized the fact that no matter how routine a situation may seem, it is always best to pray and leave nothing to chance but in the care of the Lord's capable hands.

Speaking again from my own personal experience with my own children, I can remember a recent incident with my oldest daughter, who is grown and living on her own now, that caused me to rely in the power of prayer. During the spring of 2020, she went on a humanitarian mission to South Korea to help rebuild schools that were lost in a typhoon. She was working on behalf of an organization called All Hands and Hearts that helps people all over the world that have been affected by natural disasters. Even though she kept me abreast on each leg of her journey, recognizing the power of prayer, I prayed daily as she spent nearly two weeks in a foreign land out of the reach of my direct protection. I was especially concerned for her safety because at the time of her travel, a worldwide pandemic was gripping the world and South Korea, which was considered to be one of the hot spots for a virus labeled COVID-19. I had many restless nights because, of course, all I could think of are the "what ifs," things that, in my opinion, can only truly be combated with prayer. Even after she finally landed safely back home in the United States, I still was in a state of concern and in need of the power of prayer because, as I said previously, the country she traveled to was considered highly infected with the virus COVID-19, and as such, she was immediately placed under two weeks of in-house quarantine. Remember, prayer is one of the three maintenance pillars and, in this case, not only did I praise and support her humanitarian efforts, I patiently prayed for her continued safety as she completed her mission. You see, once you become a father and adapt the attributes of a real father, you become a father for life. Far too many men think that their obligation to their children ends once they reach the magical age of eighteen as prescribed by the laws of the land, but the truth of the matter is you never stop being a real father. Notice I stressed the fact that real fathers are fathers for life because fake fathers, in far too many cases, drop their fatherly responsibilities at the time of their children's birth or during the early years of their children's development. Because they never developed a relationship with their children when they were young, they have nothing to do with them once they are grown. Unfortunately, we see this disconnect played out daily not only in real life but also in so-called reality TV shows such as the *Maury Povich Show*.

In addition, it's so sad to see a child who becomes successful under the guardianship of foster parents where they find a great role model father figure in their stepfather only to have their biological father suddenly reappear into their lives because of their success or fame. A good example of this type of scenario being played out in real life was in the case of former NBA basketball super star Shaquille O'Neal. His biological father left him and his mother in a hospital birthing room on March 6, 1972. He only showed any type of real interest in his son's life after he discovered that his son was going to appear on a TV talk show being congratulated for being drafted into the National Basketball Association (NBA) at the tender age of eighteen; he then quickly disappeared once he realized his son wasn't going to share his newfound fame and fortune with him just because he was his biological father. Then later, in typical fake father fashion, he showed up again in Shaq's life when he was nearly seventy years old after Shaq's stepfather passed away—a real man who although wasn't Shaq's biological father but in the mind of Shaq was his real father.

Finally, if we just keep in mind how our heavenly Father watches over us, He is always guiding, protecting, providing, preparing, and patiently supporting us through all of life's ups and downs; as long as we learn to pray and walk in obedience to His will and words, we will enjoy peace and joy no matter what pitfalls life throws at us. Philippians 4:6 (NIV) reminds us, "Do not be anxious about anything, but in every situation, by prayer and petition, with thanksgiving, present your requests to God."

THE SEVEN PILLARS OF FATHERHOOD

Fatherhood Quiz

1. Fill in the blank space in the following sentence. "The Lord only responds to the _____ prayers of the righteous" (James 5:16).

2. It is more important for your children's mother to pray for them because a father's primary responsibility is to provide financial support for his family.
   a. True
   b. False

3. All prayers contain four basic elements; what are they?
   a.
   b.
   c.
   d.

SURVEY RESULTS AND ANALYSIS

In an effort to gather real-world input about fatherhood, a cross sectional survey research was conducted utilizing both a closed and open-ended questionnaire (see appendix). Family members, neighbors, church members, and friends were given a set of seven closed-ended and three open-ended questions and statements. Responses to the questions and statements were obtained through emails, text messages, and handouts.

An attitude test inventory was constructed specifically for the purpose of gathering data to assess both men and women attitude toward their experience with their father or father figures.

By utilizing seven survey research rating quantifiers questions that consisted of closed-ended questions utilizing the following response categories: yes, no, sometimes, never, and all the time, information was obtained. In addition, the survey utilized three quantifiers open-ended questions requiring the survey respondents to choose the response to each question and statement that most closely described their attitude and experiences with their father or father figure.

Each of the first seven questions were constructed to determine if the respondents thought their father or father figure was a good family leader, good provider, good protector, good preparer, had patience, supportive, and was God-fearing. The last three questions were constructed to determine whether or not the respondent had a good relationship with their father or father figure, what were the best lessons the respondent's father or father figure taught them about raising children, and what characteristics and values they thought a man should have in order to be a successful father.

The sample size included fifty respondents ranging in age from twenty-one through eighty-three both male and female. This included thirty-three males and seventeen females for a total of fifty of varying ethnicities and cultural backgrounds.

In response to the question 1, "Who were you raised by?" The results were as follows:

- 62% both parents
- 26% your mother
- 2% your father
- 4% grandparents
- 6% other

In response to question 2, "Were you raised by a praying, God-fearing, and spirit-filled father?" The results were as follows:

- 44% yes (16% women vs. 28% men)
- 56% no (18% women vs. 38% men)

In response to question 3, "Do you feel your father (or father figure) provided well for you and his family?" The results were as follows:

- 62% yes
- 22% sometimes
- 16% never

In response to question 4, "When you were growing up, how often did your father tell you he loved you?" The results were as follows:

- 10% all the time
- 40% sometimes
- 50% never

In response to question 5, "When you were growing up, do you feel your father (or father figure) was supportive of your after-school activities?" The results were as follows:

- 48% yes
- 18% sometimes
- 34% never

In response to question 6, "Do you feel your father (or father figure) was a strict disciplinarian? The results were as follows:

- 58% yes
- 20% sometimes
- 22% never

In response to question 7, "Did your father (or father figure) set aside quality time for you and him to spend together?" The results were as follows:

- 30% yes
- 32% sometimes
- 38% never

In response to question 8, "Did you have a good relationship with your father while growing up, and did you or do you still have a good relationship with him now that you are grown?"

- 16% no, as an adult and as a child
- 54% yes, as an adult and as a child
- 26% no, as a child and yes, as an adult
- 4% yes, as a child and no, as an adult

In response to question 9, "What do you think was the best lesson(s) your father taught you about raising kids?" The following is a list of some of the most provocative responses:

- To have strong principles while raising children and to never falter so they never fall away from you.
- That raising kids requires an abundance of patience and positivity.
- Always treat others as you would like to be treated whether you like them or not.
- Be there for them and be involved. Refrain from criticizing them and let them grow enjoying good memories along the way.
- Perseverance, fortitude, determination, patience, commitment and hard work. Respect is a two-way street; treat people the way you would want to be treated.
- Be consistent and be a man of your word.
- Say what you mean and mean what you say by actions and deeds.
- Always be obedient to authority.
- Give them the tools to be more successful than you.
- Be a leader and a friend (leader first). Discipline when appropriate and spend quality time with your kids.
- To be proactive and consider doing the opposite of what he did as a father. Because my father was not a good father.
- The importance of listening and obeying instructions. Training up your children in the way they should go so when they get old, they will not depart from it (Proverb 22:6).
- Practice what you preach. To not teach kids that it's okay to be afraid of challenges. He believed in sayings like, "Ain't nothing to it but to do it" and "no pain no gain." He taught me to get over fears of taking risks and trying something new.
- Responsibility, accountability, and the need to create a legacy.

THE SEVEN PILLARS OF FATHERHOOD

- A father always wants his son to be better than himself; he wants him to learn from the things he's been through.
- To put God first. To always pray and give thanks for life and your blessings.
- Instill a sense of being independent and self-sufficient, help your kids expand the scope of their vision of possibilities, provide and protect your kids in fostering a safe and happy place for them to thrive, demonstrate a strong focus on family, extensions and roots help your kids' self-awareness and consciousness.
- To never settle for less and to always leave a mark on this earth and to be remembered for something amazing.
- That money doesn't grow on trees.

It is interesting to note that 20 percent of the respondents stated that their father or father figure taught them no lessons about raising children.

In response to question 10, "What characteristics and values do you think a man should have to be a successful father or father figure? The results are as follows based on the seven pillars of fatherhood:

- 22% pilot (leader) (head of household)
- 26% provider
- 6% protector
- 24% preparer (teacher) (to make ready)
- 20% praises (supporter)
- 10% patience
- 26% prays (spirit filled)
- 14% other (love, honesty, trustworthy, promise keeper, disciplinarian, etc.)

Based on the findings of this survey according to the respondents' answers to question 1, the majority stated they were raised by both parents and only by their mother. Although, some respondents stated that even though their father was present in the home, he was not an active participant in their upbringing.

Based on the findings of this survey according to the respondents' answers to question 2, the majority of the respondents stated they were not raised in a household with a God-fearing, spirit-filled father. In addition, their responses suggested that religion or a need to follow Scripture as a guidebook to lead his family never crossed their mind. In fact, most believed following the Bible and its commands was something women engaged in, not men.

Based on the findings of this survey according to the respondents' answers to question 3, the majority of the respondents stated their fathers provided well for them. It's interesting to note that this response is consistent with the attitude that most men have: the belief that all they have to do to satisfy their fatherly responsibilities is just be a good provider.

Based on the findings of this survey according to the respondents' answers to question 4, the majority of the respondents stated their fathers never told them he loved them. However, many of the respondents stated that even though their fathers didn't tell them verbally he loved them, they felt he did express he loved them by his nonverbal actions.

Based on the findings of this survey according to the respondents' answers to question 5, the majority of the respondents stated their fathers supported them when they were involved in school activities. It is also interesting to note those that stated to the contrary were very adamant that not only did their fathers not participate in their after-school activities but also, they further stated, their fathers were not present in their lives at all.

Based on the findings of this survey according to the respondents' answers to question 6, the majority of the respondents stated they felt their fathers were strict disciplinarians. In addition, most felt their fathers adopted their disciplinarian attitude from their fathers. This suggests a generational connection.

Based on the findings of this survey according to the respondents' answers to question 7, the majority of the respondents stated their fathers never set aside quality time for just them and him. And his lack of attention had a profound effect on how they perceived themselves and others.

Based on the findings of this survey according to the respondents' answers to question 8, the majority of the respondents stated they have a good relationship with their fathers while growing up and still have a good relationship with him now that they are grown; a large percentage of the respondents stated they had poor or nonexistent relationship with their father when they were growing up, but now that they have grown up, their relationship with their father has improved and continues to grow as time goes on.

Based on the findings of this survey according to the respondents' answers to question 9, although many of the respondents listed worthwhile lessons that their fathers taught them, none stated direct lessons such as being the leader/pilot or head of their family, being the protector of his children's minds and bodies, and the importance of being the spiritual guiding force in the family. All of which suggest that although many of the respondents learned some good lessons from their fathers or father figure, none learned basic foundational lessons such as the seven pillars of fatherhood.

Based on the findings of this survey according to the respondents' answers to question 10, the greatest percentages of the respondents emphasize the importance of being a good provider, teacher, and spiritually led; very few emphasize how important patience, protection, and praise are to the makeup of a real father which are vital principles in the seven pillars of fatherhood.

SOME FINAL THOUGHTS

The main component or thread that all of the seven pillars have in common is *love*. In order to truly function as a successful father is directly dependent on the amount of love you have for your family and children. Nothing should be more important than you learning to pilot and lead your family with love as your underlying driving force. Remember, if you want to pilot (lead) your family successfully, you must first love your family.

Although this book was written as a foundational guide for men and fatherhood, it is by no means intended to ignore the role and importance of women and mothers in a child's life. In the absence of a biological father or father figure in the home, many women have and continue to step up to the role of being both father and a mother to their children. However, the best family dynamic, in my opinion, is a family that has the benefits of both a father and mother who are working as a team for the greatest benefits of the family or, in the terminology of this book, a pilot and a copilot. As with the airplane pilot, his copilot is working with and alongside him to make sure the plane and its passengers arrive safely to their destinations. The copilot is always at the ready to back up the pilot no matter how rocky the flight may get and, in an emergency resulting in his inability to pilot the plane, at the ready to take the controls.

It's also interesting to note that love is the last letter in the acronym REAL, which I think denotes the most basic qualities or traits of a real father. The *R* represents *reliable*, *E* represents *engaged*, *A* represents available, and *L* represents love. All of which, of course, means a real father is a father who is a reliable person that their children can depend on to be there when they need him. So when his children are involved in a significant event in their lives such as school plays, recitals, graduations, football games, etc. and he says he will be there, he will be there. In other words, he is a promise keeper and not a promise breaker. A father who is engaged is a father who is greatly interested and committed to every aspect of his children's lives daily. That means that he knows when they need clothes; he knows their medical history. He knows their teachers, attends parent-teacher conferences, helps them with their homework, know who they hang out with at school and at play, etc. A father who is available represents a father who makes sure he set aside quality time to nurture and build lasting relationships in his children's lives. And finally, *L* represents a father who loves his children unconditionally in the same manner that our heavenly Father loves us. He understands in life, we all have made mistakes and so will his children, but he also understands he has to be there for his children when they make their mistakes ready to support and encourage them to get back on track.

I think the biblical parable of the prodigal son is a wonderful example of what can best be defined as a father who practiced agape or unconditional love for his children; as I stated in chapter 7, *patience* bears repeating. In the parable, although the father's youngest son leaves home to pursue an undisciplined sinful lifestyle, he eventually decides to return home after his sinful lifestyle catches up with him; he comes back to his father's house not knowing how his father will feel about his return. His father could have decided not to have anything to do with him and practice what we now know, in secular terms, as "tough love" and not welcome his son back into his home. But because of his love for his son and the fact that he felt that his son was once lost and now found, he instead celebrated his son's return. If we all think about it, we all may have been lost and undisciplined at one time or another as we tried to find ourselves when we were young and immature. But if we follow in the example of the prodigal son's father, we know it is more prudent to father your children with unconditional love rather than tough love. I know you may be thinking, *Didn't he use tough love when he let his son leave and he didn't try to stop him but rather let him learn the hard way what a sinful life would lead to.* Yes and no! Yes, in terms of not trying to fight his son's rebelliousness by letting his son go out into the world and learn a life lesson the tough way. And no because after the lesson was learned, he welcomed him back with open arms filled with love. Because as Scripture tells us, his son was once lost but now was found.

It's interesting to note that way too many men feel that the expression of love for their children is a function of their child's mother, especially in the case of the male child. I say this not just based on my personal opinion but also based on the survey I conducted to gather information for this book and my own personal experience with father figures I have encountered in my life. In the survey, one of the questions I asked was, When you were growing up, how often did your father tell you he loved you? And in the preponderance of the responses to this question, the answer was *never*. Even more interesting was the fact that the "never" responses came from only male respondents. Most of the female respondents either said "yes or sometimes" which was in direct contrast to the male respondents' never. There appears to be either a double standard or some unwritten macho rule that fathers should not outwardly or directly tell their male children that they love them. In fact, several male respondents stated although their fathers did not verbally express love for them, they felt that he loved them nonetheless based on his nonverbal actions. The response to this survey further indicates that many men still feel to verbally express love for their son(s) would somehow make their son(s) sissies or somehow less of a man. This is insane! And in my opinion is the reason why so many men have a difficult time developing a deep and lasting relationship with their son(s), particularly during their early years of development.

The survey also revealed another fascinating dynamic in terms of how men think of their father's love compared to how women felt about their father's love. When asked the question, Did you have a good relationship with your father while growing up, and now that you are grown, what kind of relationship do you have with him? Most of the men answered that they were not close to their father while growing up, but now that they are grown, they have developed a closer relationship with them. In contrast, most of the women answered that they had a close relationship with their fathers while they were growing up and continue to have a close relationship with them now that they are grown. This emphasizes the fact that most men, from an emotional standpoint, in most cases, raise their children with a double standard in terms of their sons and daughters. They openly display affection for their daughters but are reluctant to do the same for their sons. Perhaps this is one of the reasons why when you talk to either gender, you hear them respond to songs like Luther Vandross's "Dance With My Father" differently. For example, when my wife, Lydia, hears the song, she immediately starts thinking about her late father with tears in her eyes even though she described him as a revolving-door absentee father and sometimes an emotionally abusive father, particularly during her teen years. She also described her father as a strict disciplinarian, particularly with her only brother, while he lived with the family prior to completely abandoning his wife and kids. In contrast, in a discussion with one of the men in my neighborhood who stated that whenever he heard the song, he hated it because it brought back nothing but bad memories of a father who had abandoned his mother, him, and his siblings from the very start of his life.

Throughout this book, I have tried to stress how important the male role model is to the proper rearing of children in a family and, more importantly, the role that our heavenly Father plays in fatherhood. If you are reading this book and you are not a born-again believer, I encourage you to rethink your position on becoming a believer. I think you will find as a born-again believer, you will be changed from the inside out and will discover a whole new outlook on life that will not only be beneficial to you but also will be a blessing to your children and your family. In a research conducted by the Christian Business Men's Committee, it was found that when the father of a family was an active believer, there is about a 75 percent chance that his children will also grow up to be active believers. However, if only the mother is an active believer, the chances that the children in the family being believers goes down to 15 percent.

Remember, life is not about walking in your truth; it is about walking in God's truth. Scripture reminds us that "I have no greater joy than to hear that my children are walking in truth" (3 John 1:4

THE SEVEN PILLARS OF FATHERHOOD

NIV). And until you learn to walk in God's truth, there is no amount of money or fame that will bring you peace and joy which can only be obtained by walking in God's truth for one's life. To this day, one of my greatest regrets in life was not coming into the truth that can only be found in Christ sooner rather than later in my life.

Please note fatherhood is not just about having a child call you "Daddy." It is the journey you take with them as you guide them through life safely into maturity.

It's also important to note that there are fundamental differences in the fatherhood journey with both sons and daughters. The following are *7 Things a Son Needs from His Father* and then *7 Things a Daughter Needs from Her Father*. These seven fatherhood needs for both sons and daughters were postulated on the All Pro Dad internet blog. Note how closely they related to the seven pillars of fatherhood.

The seven things a son needs from his father are as follows:

1. *He needs you to love his mother.* By showing love for his mother, he learns how to value women and how to treat them.
2. *He needs to see you fail, not just succeed.* When your son sees you fail and handle the failure well, he sees that it is okay to make mistakes and that mistakes can be great teachers. A boy who is not afraid of making mistakes will grow into a man positioned to accept and conquer great challenges.
3. *He needs your servant leadership.* Your son needs to see leadership in your home. He needs to see you leading by serving; he will better understand leadership and be able to more effectively lead versus follow his peers.
4. *He needs you to be present.* He needs you to be present in his education, in his social life, in all areas of his life.
5. *He needs your love regardless of his choices.* Just as the Father of all fathers, our heavenly Father, offers us unconditional love regardless of our choices, we should always afford our sons unconditional love no matter how bad their choices.
6. *He needs you to affirm him.* Through praise and support, a son's self-esteem is bolstered and reinforced. Studies have

shown that when fathers are affectionate and supportive, it greatly affects a child's cognitive and social development. It also instills an overall sense of well-being and self-confidence.
7. *He needs you to discipline him in love.* Disciplining him in love will teach him to consider the consequences his actions will have. This will prepare him to think and evaluate the choices he makes both now and in the future.

The seven things a daughter needs from her father are as follows:

1. *She needs you to be involved.* Show your daughter you are interested in her life by learning more about it and trying to become a part of it.
2. *She needs you to demonstrate a healthy marriage.* A father that displays physical affection, respect, and a true partnership with his wife provides an incredible example that his daughter will want to mirror in her own life.
3. *She needs you to support her.* When a father fully supports his daughter, she will develop a strong self-esteem and a positive self-image.
4. *She needs to trust you as a confidante.* When your daughter discusses personal issues or problems, treat them with respect and confidence.
5. *She needs your unconditional love.* Just as our Father in heaven demonstrates unconditional love, fathers on earth need to display this as well.
6. *She needs a strong spiritual leader.* A father should be the spiritual head of a household and should take charge of his children's religious education.
7. *She needs a positive role model.* A daughter's father sets the standard for all other men in her life, and a positive role model helps her to choose a good husband. Her father is the first man in her life that she will intimately know.

A real father must remember that they cannot model perfection because we are not perfect; real fathers can only model growth. Their children need to know that they are always in the process of becoming Christlike and in the likeness of their heavenly Father.

Your children need to see how you, their father, handle failure as well as how you handle success. When a father models this kind of honesty, he is not only demonstrating the attributes of a real father but also greatly reduces the possibility of the devil gaining control of his children.

Remember, in the words of Stephen Colbert, "A father has to be a provider, a teacher, a role model, but most importantly a distant authority figure who can never be pleased otherwise, how will children ever understand the concept of God." This is in line with a scripture that reminds us, "My son, do not despise the Lord's discipline, and do not resent his rebuke, because the Lord disciplines the one, he loves, and he chastens everyone he accepts as his son" (Hebrews 12:6 NIV).

CONCLUSION

When it is all said and done, you must ask yourself, As a father, what will be my greatest legacy that I will leave with my children? Will it be one that will set them on a path of success in life or one of failure?

In the search of the fundamental traits or pillars of what true fatherhood really looks like, we first explored the attributes of what a fake father or, what I like to term, "man-child" looks like.

Then in chapter 1, "The Importance of Fatherhood," fatherhood driven by godly principles such as the seven pillars of fatherhood was explored. In basic terms, to be a successful father, every man must understand and realize that he must seek out and be led by the Holy Spirit—the father of all righteousness and fatherly wisdom.

Without a strong godly father figure in a child's life, they are left with nothing more than distorted ideas and perceptions of what a real father looks like. These are distorted ideas and perceptions that include how to accept responsibility, how to relate to and treat properly the opposite sex, how to manage money, how to raise children, and, most importantly, how to look always to their heavenly Father for guidance and direction. These distorted fatherhood figures are driven by what men see in the media and advice from other men with distorted ideas on fatherhood. Ideals such as all a man really is obligated to do for his family and children is to "bring home the bacon," and anything more than this is the responsibility of their mothers. They were never taught or demonstrated that a real man must step up and be led by the Lord as the head or leader of his family; they had to not only provide but also prepare and protect their children. They had to be patient, supportive, and loving toward their children and that they should always lift up their children in prayer in all circumstances. If these things are not done, they will not only fail their children but also will also risk failure in terms of what a real father looks like in the eyes of the Father of all fathers—our heavenly Father.

Further, in chapter 1, the importance in recognizing that the core value of any society begins and ends with the family unit was discussed. And at the center of any family unit is a father or father figure. And even if, for whatever reason, the biological father or father figure is not present or available, our heavenly Father is always present and ready to step in with guidance and directions that will help lead a family on a path of righteousness. Although this guidance and directions is always available, far too many men ignore this gift from their heavenly Father and opt instead to follow the misguided attributes of a fake father.

One of the greatest needs of any family is a father or father figure that is passionately committed to the responsibility of being a real father. This, I think, can best be summed up even more simply by the acronym REAL. This means that a real father must be *r*eliable, *e*ngaged, *a*vailable, and *l*oving. To be real, to be engaged, to be available, and to be loving can be expressed by all fathers who learn to embrace and practice the seven pillars of fatherhood as outlined in this book.

In chapter 2, "Pillar 1—The Pilot Father," "pilot-leader" was discussed. Being the first of the seven pillars and one of the four foundational pillars, it sets the stage for the next three foundational pillars which dictate how a father will shape his children's views and attitudes to each of the challenges they will face in terms of the seven dimensions of human endeavors. In other words, will their spiritual, physical, nutritional, social, emotional, intellectual, and financial endeavors in life match a father whose values and attitude, hopefully, are based on these attributes of a real father and not a fake father.

To illustrate the importance of the pilot-leader in the family, an airplane pilot example was utilized. The idea that just as an airplane pilot is responsible for all of his passengers and dictates their safe travel to a given location, so it is with the pilot-leader of his family who is responsible for all members of his family's well-being. In addition, he must navigate their safe travel through different phases of their lives.

And in the same way that a bad pilot can crash his plane into a mountain without proper guidance and directions jeopardizing all his passengers on board, so it is with a fake father pilot-leader who, without proper guidance and directions, will crash his family and children into a mountain of a life full of destruction, failure, and despair.

In chapter 3, "Pillar 2—The Provider Father," provider fathers were discussed emphasizing the fact that it is the second of the four pillars that make up the maintenance pillars; statistically speaking, it appears to be one of the pillars that most men feel that is the only thing that a father is obligated to do in terms of raising their children.

This chapter also emphasized the fact that all real fathers should remember that fatherhood is an important obligation, and no man should bring a child into this world if they cannot properly provide for them. Let's face it: if you can barely take care of yourself, what sense does it make for you to subject a child to your limited resources? As I stated in the chapter, and it bears repeating, if you cannot afford them (children), think twice even three times before you make them!

The chapter concluded with seven key focal points:

Point number 1. Always remember that providing financially for your children is a basic responsibility that all real men embrace without question.
Point number 2. Always remember that providing for your children is a basic responsibility, but it is also extremely important to provide your children with time and attention.
Point number 3. Always remember that your children want your love and respect.
Point number 4. Always remember that you never stop providing for your children even after they become adults.
Point number 5. Always remember your children are always seeking your approval.

Point number 6. Always remember you are a king in your children's eyes. And as their king, they import their values and morals from you.

Point number 7. Finally, always remember, as a wise man once taught me, there is no such thing as illegitimate children, only illegitimate parents.

In chapter 4, "Pillar 3—The Protector Father," protector father was discussed which stressed the fact that all real fathers recognize the need to protect their children from the predators of life. This includes not only those predators that may harm their children physically but, just as important, those that may harm their children emotionally.

The chapter utilized the acronym PET to emphasize the fact that all real fathers should be on the lookout for (P) *peer pressure* predators, (E) *environmental* peer pressure predators, (T) *themselves* or self-image peer pressure.

The chapter concluded with a warning that a real father's protection of his children starts from the time they are in their mother's womb and throughout their lives. A real father recognizes that even when their children are in the womb, he must provide protection for his mate's health and safety throughout their pregnancy. And once they are born, he should be on guard for things such as sudden infant death syndrome (SID), otherwise known as crib death.

Finally, the chapter noted a study that was conducted by Michigan State University which found that a father's relationship with their children from toddler through fifth grade was important in their children's health and development.

In chapter 5, "Pillar 4—The Preparing Father," the preparing father pillar stressed the fact that all real fathers must prepare and teach their children to go forth into the world with skills and abilities in seven areas of human endeavors; these include the spiritual, physical, nutritional, social, emotional, intellectual, and financial. If these fundamental principles of endeavors are not taught by a father or father figure, then the responsibility will fall on their children's mothers or grandparents or, in far too many cases to the detriment of the child, social media and the streets (in the form of gangs, etc.).

In terms of your children's spiritual well-being and development, it's first and foremost the man of the house responsibility to introduce his children to the Creator of all things. A real father knows the best way to do this is by way of example. He understands that if his children see him openly praying with the family, regularly attending church, and participating in church activities, it will have a profound effect on their spiritual walk since a child sees a real father as their greatest hero, and all children deep down want to be like their hero. Notice I said a real father and not a fake father. Fake fathers, in far too many cases, cause their children to despise and distrust them, and by no means are they their children's hero. I passionately believe a life not based on a sound spiritual foundation is life doomed to failure.

In terms of his children's physical well-being and development, it's a real father's responsibility to teach and show his children how to take care of themselves physically. Exercise and proper grooming habits for the most part are some things that are not innate in children; they are learned behaviors. In other words, they are not just things your children teach themselves; they must learn them from their father/father figure or from an outside source such as their peer group or what they gleam from social media. They learn these things from their father by way of example and instructions.

A real father must teach his children how to stay physically fit by encouraging them to get involved in activities such as dancing, aerobics, bike riding, football, basketball, tennis, etc.—things that will be beneficial in keeping their bodies fit and healthy.

In addition, a real father must teach his children that life is full of physical ups and downs. And because of these ups and downs, the more they need to prepare ahead of time for the rigors of life by taking good care of themselves physically as well as being prepared to face what I like call DAGE. Dage is an acronym that stands for decay-aging-genetics-environment. In other words, as long as we live and breathe, we will be subject to constant decay, the aging process that is governed by time, genetic markers we inherit from our parents, and the environment with all of its toxins and pollution.

In terms of nutrition, the chapter addressed the fact that it is the responsibility of a real father to teach his children how to properly fuel their bodies by eating food that is not simply good tasting but food that is good for them. If their children see their father, who again is seen as their number one hero and example, eating junk food on the regular, then it should come as no surprise that his children will adapt the same behavior or eating pattern.

In terms of the social, the chapter addressed the fact that without your preparation and guidance, your children could possibly live out their lives daily in social/emotional realms of reacting to and operating off on horizontal stimuli such as social media that directly affects their emotional well-being.

The chapter also pointed out that all real fathers must prepare their children for life by limiting their children's exposure time to video games, TV, and cell phones. They recognize that the best way to get their children away from these destructive habits is to schedule quality family time with his children—quality time that includes but not limited to family activities such as game night and date nights with just him and them.

In terms of the emotional, all real fathers must be ready to emotionally prepare their children by, first and foremost, providing them with a stable and loving home environment. If a man's children see love being displayed between their parents, and their parents are constantly expressing love for them, then they will grow up with a sense of self-assurance and love for themselves and others. In addition, as stated previously, the chapter emphasized the fact that all real fathers recognize that they must prepare and teach their children how to emotionally cope with life's ups and downs. If a father properly prepares his children on how to deal with life's storms by developing an attitude that is founded and grounded in Scripture that reminds us to worry about nothing and to pray about everything, they will be able to maintain a sense of emotional stability no matter what life throws at them.

The chapter also emphasized that it must be born in every real father's mind that the intellectual starts while their children are still in their mother's womb and continues for the rest of their lives under

THE SEVEN PILLARS OF FATHERHOOD

a father's guidance and support. A real father must consider how they are going to fund their children's educational pursuits among other things such as the pros and the cons in terms of home schooling, public schooling, or private schooling. Each, of course, has both advantages and disadvantages. To properly prepare children intellectually, just as stated previously, in the social requires a father who understands the benefits of restricting their children's access to unproductive activities such as too much TV watching, cell phone activities, and video game playing.

In terms of the financial, the chapter explored how a real father must prepare his children in the proper managing of their finances. It's the duty of every parent, and particularly the father figure in their lives, to empower their children with financial wisdom. This financial wisdom starts with teaching their children first by example and then by instructions on how to budget and the importance of staying out of debt and, finally, how to save and invest for long-term security.

In chapter 6, "Pillar 5—The Praising Father," the praising pillar was discussed. In this chapter, the importance of how praise and encouragement impacted upon the children's self-esteem was highlighted. The chapter pointed to the fact that real fathers recognize that a healthy self-esteem helps their children feel secure and worthwhile. It helps them to build positive relationships with others and feel confident about their God-given abilities. A healthy self-esteem also helps his children to be opened to learning and feedback which can help them acquire and master new skills.

The chapter also pointed to research that indicated praise and encouragement helps children to accomplish general everyday task. Research further showed that children can become self-motivated when their natural curiosity is encouraged and supported. And they tend to do things simply because they enjoy doing them. In addition, all real fathers need to be on guard from negatively influencing their children's motivation by making them feel they need a reward every time they do something right. Praise is more effective when it is specific and when parents and loved ones are mindful of how and when they praise. Praise should be given mindfully considering a child's age, stage of development, and their individual ability. Timing of praise is also important because interrupting a child when they are concentrating can make them lose their motivation to continue with a given activity.

The chapter also offered seven helpful tips to utilize when it comes to building your children's self-esteem which included the following:

- When you feel good about your child, say so.
- Always be on the lookout for small changes and accomplishments.
- Try not to practice a leave alone zap attitude toward your children.
- Recognize that not everyone is the same.
- You should praise your child for their unique strengths.
- Encourage them to develop and feel excited about their interest.
- Surprise your children with rewards for good behavior.
- Praise effort as well as achievement.
- Try to make praise dependent on your children's behavior rather than your feelings.

In the case of the female child, the chapter reminded fathers that she has an innate need to be affirmed by a male figure, particularly in her formative years; if she doesn't get that affirmation from her father or father figure, her self-esteem in many cases can suffer. In the case of the male child, fathers were reminded that the greatest praise a son can get is from his earthly father. And all real fathers should never underestimate the importance in being involved in the major events of their children's lives.

The chapter ended with a caution and a warning against criticizing and overly praising. Studies have shown that not only is too much praise harmful to a child's self-esteem but also criticizing children, particularly during their formative years, was unhealthy and can adversely affect their self-esteem.

In chapter 7, "Pillar 6—The Patient Father," patience was discussed. We found that patience was more than just a virtue and that haste makes waste. And when it comes to raising children, patience takes on a whole new meaning because raising children requires not only patience but also understanding. As a real father, it's important to know the difference between alienating your children and firmly directing them with a spiritually derived perspective. This chapter also reminded us that when the man of the house loses control, the whole house is out of control. An angry, out of control father must learn how to step back, cool down, and consult the Father of all fathers, our heavenly Father, or his anger can and will bring out the worst in him with life-changing consequences; Scripture reminds us, "Fathers, do not provoke your children to anger by the way you treat them. Rather bring them up with discipline and instruction that comes from the Lord" (Ephesian 6:4 NLT).

This chapter goes on to point out the fact that patience is closely related to discipline. All fathers must recognize that in order to direct his children away from disobedience, he must learn to use punishment at the correct time and situation. No matter what the age of his child, when it comes to their discipline, a father must keep in mind that their discipline is causally related to how their father practice and embraces patience and that true discipline is always coupled with unconditional love and patience.

Finally, this chapter ends with an admonishment that all godly directed real fathers must continually strive to understand their children's greatest strengths and weaknesses. And he must strive to be a father who recognizes his children's possible beginnings and ends but still wise enough and patient enough not to force his will on his children.

In chapter 8, "Pillar 7—The Praying Father," we learned why it was so important that all real fathers learn why and how to become a prayer warrior on behalf of their children.

The prayer pillar is the third and final maintenance pillar. It is the pillar that all fathers must learn and utilize throughout their children's lives regardless of their age. This chapter also defined prayer and outlined eight key effectual prayer components that include the following: (1) know to whom you are speaking, (2) thank the Lord, (3) ask for God's will, (4) say what you need, (5) ask for forgiveness, (6) pray with a friend, (7) pray the Word, and (8) memorize Scripture.

Since prayer should not only be effectual but also come from those that are fervent and righteous, both fervent and righteous were defined.

The chapter concluded with a look at the use of the word *acts* as an acronym that reminds us of the basic elements of prayer. With the *A* in acts representing *adoration*, the *C* representing *confession*, *T* representing *thanksgiving*, and *S* representing *supplication*.

When it's all said and done, you'll know you have become a real father after skillfully applying the principles as set forth by the seven pillars of fatherhood when your children lovingly refer to you as "my pops, my dad, or my daddy." And one of best gifts that I received on one Father's Day was a desk plaque that says, "I'm a dad; what's your superpower?"

So I will leave you with this question, Are you or will you be your children's superpower?

APPENDIX

Fatherhood Survey

1. Who were you raised by?
   A. Both parents
   B. Your father
   C. Your mother
   D. Grandparents
   E. Other

2. Were you raised by a praying, God-fearing, and spirit-filled father?
   A. Yes
   B. No

3. Do you feel your father or father figure provided well for you and his family?
   A. Yes
   B. Sometimes
   C. Never

4. When you were growing up, how often did your father tell you he loved you?
   A. All the time
   B. Sometime
   C. Never

5. When you were growing up, do you feel your father or father figure was supportive of your after-school activities?
   A. Yes
   B. Sometimes
   C. Never

6. Do you feel your father or father figure was a strict disciplinarian?
   A. Yes
   B. Sometimes
   C. Never

7. Did your father or father figure set aside quality time for you and him to spend together?
   A. Yes
   B. Sometimes
   C. Never

8. Did you have a good relationship with your father while growing up and continued to have a good relationship with him after you were grown?

9. What do you think was the best lesson(s) your father taught you about raising kids?

10. What characteristics and values do you think a man should have to be a successful father or father figure?

SUGGESTED READING

1. *Fathered by God* by John Eldredge (Thomas Nelson)
2. *You Have What It Takes* by John Eldredge (Thomas Nelson)
3. *Talking with My Father* by Ray C. Stedman (Discovery House)
4. *God Needs Some Boots on the Ground* by Yevette Cashwell (Xulon Press)
5. *Trusting God in Hard Times* y Bill Crowder (Discovery House)
6. *The Bondage Breaker* by Neil T. Anderson (Harvest House)
7. *Seven Dimensions of Human Endeavors* by Donald H. Wood (Covenant Books Inc.)

ABOUT THE AUTHOR

Donald H. Wood, PhD is a devoted member and vice chairman trustee at his local church in Waldorf, Maryland, where he loves to worship and serve his Lord and Savior Jesus Christ. He is the husband of Lydia and the father of Adriel and Kristin. He has authored the book *Seven Dimensions of Human Endeavors* and is a former adjunct assistant professor with the Universities of Maryland and the District of Columbia. He has earned multiple degrees that cover the disciplines of psychology and human resource development.

CPSIA information can be obtained
at www.ICGtesting.com
Printed in the USA
BVHW032321180422
634471BV00001B/47